# a girl and her greens

ALSO BY APRIL BLOOMFIELD

*A Girl and Her Pig*

# a girl and her greens
## hearty meals from the garden

## APRIL BLOOMFIELD

### with JJ GOODE

*photographs by david loftus*

*illustrations by sun young park*

CANONGATE

Published in 2015 by Canongate Books Ltd,
14 High Street, Edinburgh EH1 1TE

www.canongate.tv

1

First published in the USA by Ecco, an imprint of HarperCollins
Publishers, 10 East 53rd Street, New York, NY 10022

*British Library Cataloguing-in-Publication Data*
A catalogue record for this book is available on request from the
British Library

ISBN 978 1 78211 170 2

*Designed by Suet Yee Chong*

Printed and bound in Slovenia by GPS

# contents

# acknowledgements

Let's start with the most important person: thank you to Louis Russo, the young man who came up with the title for this book!

Thank you to the amazing team at Ecco, especially Dan Halpern, Gabriella Doob, Libby Edelson, Suet Chong, Allison Saltzman and Rachel Meyers, for helping me create a book that I adore. And best of luck at your new job, Libby.

To my superstar agent, the always dapper Luke Janklow.

To my friend and co-writer, JJ Goode, for driving me nuts, making me measure, and making me laugh.

To my friend, the brilliant photographer David Loftus, and food and prop stylist Georgie ('Puddin' and Pi') Socratous and Irene Wong for helping me make this book beautiful.

To Sun Young Park for her incredible illustrations.

To my friend Martin Schoeller for yet another lovely cover photo.

To Amy Vogler and Marian Bull for their careful, thoughtful recipe testing.

To Jamie Oliver, Pete Begg and Dolly Sweet for their advice, support and friendship.

To my friend and partner Ken Friedman. When shall we open another one?

To my hardworking and patient assistant, SarahGlenn Bernstein.

To my wonderful staff, who kept everything humming away while I worked on this book. Special thanks to Katharine Marsh, Christina Lecki, Josh Even, Ryan Jordan, Amy Hess, Robert Flaherty, Charlene Santiago, Jimbo Gibson, Edie Ugot and Peter Cho.

To Amy Hou, my rock.

# introduction

I've developed a bit of a reputation for meat, particularly the odd parts – what I call the not-so-nasty bits. I certainly do adore trotters and kidneys and liver. I get chuffed about a roast dinner or sticky veal shank or a good burger. Yet lamb shoulders and suckling pigs are sort of like action films, with lots of explosions and excitement. You like them, but you probably don't want to watch them *all* the time. And not even the juiciest steak or crispiest pig's ear gets me happy like nice peas.

Just about my favourite thing to do is go to the farmers' market in spring in search of flawless pea pods, unblemished and full. I walk around like a kid in a sweet shop, nabbing a pod at my favourite stall, gently squeezing until it splits to reveal a happy row of peas, and popping one in my mouth. You know when you like something so much that it makes you not just nod your head in satisfaction, but shake your head in disbelief? That's what happens when I find that perfectly sweet pea. So many things conspired to make that pea – the weather, the soil, the farmer – and there you are on the receiving end. It makes me happy and grateful.

And I love that later on, I know I'll be propped up at the counter with my big bag of peas, gently squeezing their bottoms so the pods pop open, running my finger along each one to split them, and nudging the peas into a bowl, listening to the pitter-patter sound they make as they tumble in. If I ever get up the nerve to get a tattoo, I'll get one that shows a few pretty green pods.

I didn't exactly grow up on a farm. I grew up in Birmingham and, like most big cities, it's a place dominated by concrete and shopping centres.

I was as particular an eater then as I am today. While nowadays I get fussy about finding the sweetest peas and the prettiest carrots, back when I was little, I got fussy about liking my bacon sandwiches with the slices still a bit floppy and a good dose of HP sauce. I insisted on eating my fish-finger sandwiches with butter and ketchup. When my nan skewered pineapple and cheddar chunks for a party, as people used to back then, I'd always steal the pineapple but leave the cheddar. To eat my Cadbury Flake, I'd squeeze the long package to crumble up the chocolate, then I'd open one side and tip it all into my mouth at once.

Like many working-class people, my parents didn't always have time to shop for fresh vegetables, let alone peel them. I ate plenty of cauliflower, broccoli, and carrots that came from freezer bags. I'd cram these horrible veg into my cheeks like a chipmunk does, because I knew I had to eat them but I wanted to delay the chewing and the tasting. Frozen peas, however, I loved. I still do.

When the vegetables were fresh, they were often cooked in the English manner of the times – that is, for too long, until they were squishy and a little grey. I still remember some godawful Brussels sprouts, which at the time I just loved, boiled to buggery in a pressure cooker. England has come a long way since then.

We'd occasionally eat marrow, a sort of watery, overgrown courgette, as big as my forearm. My mom would scrape out the seedy middles to make canoes, pack in minced meat, and bake them. I quite liked these, the way the marrow got creamy and you could just shovel it into your mouth with the meat without thinking that you were eating the vegetable. For a spell in the '80s, after we moved house and got our first microwave, my family lived on potatoes 'baked' in the futuristic oven. Imagine, putting something as lovely as a potato in the microwave! Even as a girl, I knew how wonderful potatoes could be, thanks to my school's cafeteria. I might have been horrible at my times tables – while the rest of the class was on 6s, I could barely make it through my 2s – but I was quite good at eating steamy boiled potatoes bombarded with butter and black pepper.

My early vegetable mentors weren't chefs obsessed with the

perfect tomato or blokes who plunged their hands into the cool dirt to pull up carrots. One of them was my granddad. When I was a girl, he ran a small café called Lincon Road. His customers were a mix of Mods and Rockers. Mods wore suits with thin ties, rode mopeds, and listened to dub music and The Who; Rockers wore leather, rode proper motorcycles, and listened to Elvis and Eddie Cochrane. When the two factions weren't fighting each other, they were trying to drill a hole in the café's pinball machine to get at the coins inside. My granddad tried to keep the peace with tea and toast.

He loved his café. And he was a good cook. He was particularly proud of the fry-ups he cooked there, which along with the mandatory egg, bread, sausage, and bacon included lowly vegetables like button mushrooms, Heinz tinned baked beans, and pale tomato halves browned slightly in hot fat. While I loved the meaty bits, I had special affection for those tomatoes. Just when you thought you couldn't take another bite of sausage, the tomatoes' acidity would revive your palate and you'd go back in for more.

My nan, who passed away more than a decade ago, also put thought and attention into her vegetable cookery. She made the best Sunday roast, which was less about the lamb or pork she made than it was about the unromantic array of carrots, parsnips, peas, sprouts, potatoes and swedes – none of the Treviso, ramps and Romanesco that get me giddy these days. The pile on my plate, so high it nearly reached my chin, was mostly veg. She was really good with mise en place: growing up, I delighted in visiting her house and seeing the stove arranged with little pots, each filled with peeled vegetables ready to be cooked.

My mom might not have been the world's greatest cook, but she did have a little garden. My parents didn't have much money, but they were quite house-proud and always kept our modest terrace house in Druid's Heath looking nice. In the garden, my mom planted pretty little plots of pansies and strawberries, tomatoes, and spring onions. I loved the taste of her tomatoes straight off the vine, though when she made salad with those same tomatoes and her spring onions, I'd still douse the whole thing with Heinz Salad Cream, like a proper kid. I wish everyone had their own garden. I wish I had my own garden. In New York City, I don't even have a pot on the fire escape.

Things changed after I finished my first cooking job, at the carvery station at a Holiday Inn. I was lucky to work for chefs with an affection for produce, like Rowley Leigh and Simon Hopkinson. But my own affection for veg really took off when I started at the River Café, working for Rose Gray and Ruth Rogers.

I was swept up by all of their obsessions, especially the vegetables that they sourced from Italy. There were proper Florence fennel and artichokes and celeriac that Rose and Ruth brought in by the pallet. Until then, these were things I liked all right but didn't really understand. I knew celeriac to be a pleasant, if unremarkable, root whose main distinction was that it was knobby, and a bit homely. Not at the River Café. There it was dense and sweet. A sniff at the base would yield that floral aroma, just as it would when I sniffed a ripe melon.

Besides rediscovering old friends, I also met new ones, like the Roman delicacy called puntarelle, a highly seasonal chicory whose slender leaves are very, very bitter. Because Rose and Ruth adored it, I ate it again and again in order to understand the pleasure they took in it, in the same way you want to try lager because your dad drinks it, then next thing you know you see past the bitterness and actually enjoy it yourself.

After five years at the River Café, I moved to Berkeley, California. The first day I arrived at my flat on Shattuck and Folsom, I was too chuffed to just sit around, so I dropped my bags and had a wander. I didn't know my way, but next thing I knew, I was staring at a big peace sign made out of garlic heads hanging on a gate outside a restaurant. I had stumbled on Chez Panisse, where I had come to work. My new boss was Chris Lee, and his kitchen was filled with people who had been cooking there for ten years. That told me a lot about the place, straight away. Jobs in restaurant kitchens are typically high-turnover, because of the intensity of the work, the low pay, and cranky-knickers bosses like yours truly; but there, no one seemed to ever want to leave.

Chez Panisse, if you haven't heard, was a pioneer in simple, ingredient-driven cooking. Working there, you couldn't help but develop a close connection to the ingredients at hand. In fact, part of the job was learning how they were grown. That's how I came to visit Green String Farm (then called Cannard Farm) in Sonoma County, which supplied much of the produce we cooked with at Chez Panisse. I met an engaging man called Bob Cannard, who taught me how much work and passion it takes to grow wonderful vegetables. I learned that not all soil is created equal and that you could alter its mineral composition (Bob enriched it with pulverized oyster shells, old crops left to die, and something he called 'compost tea') to give the vegetables what they needed to grow and be tasty. I learned that bugs weren't necessarily the enemies of vegetables. Bob considered bugs to be helpful little critters – seeing them ravaging a plant told him that the plant itself wasn't healthy enough to ward off the fellows. It's funny, but toiling in a windowless restaurant kitchen, it's surprisingly easy to forget that vegetables come from seeds in the ground and not from boxes brought by your purveyor.

I might never have left California with its vast variety of produce, available almost all year round, if I hadn't been offered the job at the Spotted Pig. I'm happy I did leave, if only because I like the East Coast and its more dramatic seasons. Every time you turn around, there's something new to be excited about: Ooh, ramps are coming in! Fantastic, pumpkin is back!

One of the loveliest things about vegetables is their ability to evoke a particular season or place. Meat and seafood can do this, too – there's spring lamb, softshell crabs, and shad roe – but nothing like how a heap of ramps at the farmers' market announces spring's arrival or how endless punnets of tomatoes on a table at a roadside stall signal summer. When the leaves begin to turn, you won't spot aubergines at the market. When you're still wearing your thermals, you won't find spring garlic, with their purple-speckled bulbs and pert green stalks, no matter how hard you search. And that's OK. In fact, I quite like it.

Life would be boring if you could have everything at any time. I like the limits that the seasons impose. I like having something to look forward to. I don't even mind when nature disappoints me with a bad year for corn or tomatoes. You develop an almanac in your head – like, 'Oh, tomatoes were so bad that year.' When great ones return, you get to think, 'Finally, lovely tomatoes!' Vegetables make you happy when they're there, and you miss them when they're gone.

When I told a friend that I was working on a vegetable cookbook, he said that this made sense, since vegetables have become so trendy. I had a good laugh at that. I guess I must have lost the plot somewhere along the way, because I still don't think beetroot, carrots and asparagus are cool. I do, however, think that they're delicious. That's good enough for me.

But I suppose I see what my mate meant. Lately, you've got people like Michael Pollan and Mark Bittman making the case with science and common sense that we should all cut back on meat, for our health as well as for the planet's. Chefs have been taking up the cause, treating veg with the love and care once reserved mainly for rib eye steaks and lamb chops. My motivation is more about passion than scruples. I'm not trying to make a statement. I just love the way boiled broccoli raab sort of bites the back of your mouth. I love how creamy properly cooked aubergine gets. I could shuck corn all day, thinking about how sweet it'll taste.

Vegetables have some practical advantages over meat, too. For example, while pork shoulders and legs of lamb need to be cooked softly, you're not going to braise an artichoke for hours. Still, I don't like to think of cooking, eating, and enjoying vegetables as something you do while you're not eating meat. While this book is about vegetables, not all the recipes are vegetarian. I like cooking my collards with lots of bacon. Anchovies give so many veg a lift. Some vegetables even turn meaty on you. Red onion gives sauces and soups a meatiness that other onions don't. Mushrooms give off an inviting aroma as they sear, which makes me think of veal kidneys. Artichoke hearts have a fleshy texture. Boiled asparagus can be juicy. I'm not saying vegetables should aspire to be like meat. I'm just saying that meat eaters will appreciate these qualities, and that vegetables *can* satisfy you the way meat does.

## the farmers' market

Before you cook, you must shop, and there's no better place to shop than the farmers' market. Your goal is to find the best vegetables that you can. The higher your standards, the better your food will be.

First off, have a brisk walk through the market without buying a thing. This is especially true for markets that are new to you, where you don't know the vendors well. Because while it's tempting to jump at the first bunch of radishes you spot, not all veg, no matter how lovingly they're grown, are the same. What a shame it would be to buy radishes at one stall only to come across even perter, more peppery ones elsewhere. You want to make your walk brisk – really get a wiggle on! – so you can get back to any bunches and baskets that struck you earlier, before they get snapped up.

If you have the opportunity to taste what you see, please do, though you should ask your farmer nicely first. Taste everything you can. In the summer, taste cherry tomatoes until you find those that are thrillingly sweet-tart and explode when you bite them. In the spring, taste peas. I like to visit every stand and ogle the bins of peas, looking for the prettiest ones. Then I'll pick out a nice plump pod and pinch it open. Pop a pea in your mouth. If it's candy sweet and barely starchy, grab a bag and fill it up. Taste rocket from this stall and that until you find the one that aggressively bites the sides of your tongue.

Have a chat with a farmer. You might learn that her pumpkins are especially sweet thanks in part to a frost. She might turn you on to an oddball mushroom that she tells you tastes a bit like crab, or you might encounter so-called over-wintered broccoli raab, which is especially sweet. And don't forgot to snap pictures of celebrity vegetables, such as the hard-to-find Rosa Bianca variety of aubergine (squat and ridged with mottled light purple and white skin), so you can look at them during a dull moment in your day or while planning a dinner, and get reinvigorated.

It should go without saying that you should never pick anything that's bruised, spongy or bendy. But perfect-looking vegetables don't always taste perfect. Selecting great vegetables comes with experience. When you taste something at the market, or later as you're cooking, take a close look at it. Wonder what was it about this courgette – perhaps it was a big honking thing – that might have warned you that it would taste so bland. What was it about this tomato – perhaps it was evenly coloured, even near the stem, and heavy for its size – that could have told you it would be so sweet and meaty?

This way, you'll develop preferences. One of my preferences, in general, is for small to medium-size vegetables. I don't care for spindly, sprouty asparagus, but I'm not into fat stalks either. Tiny courgettes are adorable, but so small that you don't get to enjoy the vegetable's character. I could live without baby fennel, which is too small to serve as crunchy slices or to be boiled to a creamy, meaty texture. Large pea pods seem tempting until you realize that the biggest ones tend to be starchy. While you might be tempted by a massive carrot, thinking you'd only have to peel that one, keep in mind that smaller carrots tend to taste sweeter and have thin skin that you don't need to peel at all.

Certain vegetables need to be used as soon as possible. Peas, corn, and green beans are sweetest just after they're picked. As they sit, the sugars turn to starch. So when you find sweet corn at the market, cook it for dinner that night.

Of course, vegetables don't always cooperate. Then you must adapt. If you'd like to make salad but the tomatoes are nearly bursting from the skins, consider making sauce instead. If you can't find tomatoes that meet your standard, change your plans on what to cook for dinner. You never want to go to the market stubborn.

## the simple things

Often I find that the least exciting way of cooking actually leads to the most wonderful place. In fact, I like lots of vegetables – artichokes, Brussels sprouts, cauliflower – just boiled in salty water and served with a glug of olive oil and a sprinkle of chilli or a tender squeeze of lemon. If you've got perfect veg, there's no need to manipulate it. There's nothing wrong with finding broccoli raab and just blanching it. Maybe you're thinking, 'Blanched broccoli, that sounds like the worst thing in the world.' But if your product is amazing and you don't cook it to buggery, then just blanching it can be the most beautiful thing.

In fact, part of me thinks that unless you're a practised home cook, you should treat all vegetables like this, though a list of stuff I like to boil wouldn't make for much of a cookbook, now would it? Nor would it go over well at my restaurants if I served only plates of boiled swede and boiled carrots. That's why in this cookbook most of the recipes go much further than plain old boiling.

Yet because the simplest preparations deserve attention as well, I've sprinkled throughout the book a handful of not quite recipes for some of my favourite vegetables. I wanted to share with you the way I eat ingredients like tomatoes, corn, and potatoes at home, when I don't have to please anyone but myself. They're so simple that they don't require full-on recipes. Instead, they're more like little road maps encouraging you to play around and find your own way. Whatever you do, you want your potatoes to still taste like potatoes, your corn to still taste like corn. Whatever you add – lemon, chilli, anchovy, or all three – shouldn't dominate. These kinds of flavour enhancers should help bring out the good qualities of the veg or serve to balance its harsh ones.

My hope is that you'll start playing with vegetables on your own. Take fennel, lovely fennel. When it's raw, it has a soft crunch and subtle anise-y sweetness. When you boil the fennel, its texture goes creamy and its sweetness really comes out to say hello. You don't *have to* do anything more but sometimes it's good fun to continue to transform the flavour, though never so much that you obscure the essence of the fennel itself. Maybe you decide to go that extra step and concentrate that sweetness by sautéing the boiled fennel, then balancing that sweetness with a little acidity – a splash of vinegar or tart citrus. If you're feeling ambitious, you might start exploring different sides of the same vegetable, combining raw and roasted fennel.

Never neglect the simple pleasures of cooking. When recipes do require more than a dunk in boiling water, try not to look at the process as a chore. If you think about how slow-cooked onions will ultimately transform a dish, the work itself becomes exciting. Get to know the process. Many of my recipes begin the same way, with onions and perhaps garlic or carrots sweating in hot fat. Settle in at the stove while they sizzle. Stir them and watch closely as they change. As you stir, look out for the point they begin to stick to the pan ever so slightly, which happens right before browning begins. Taste them, so you can see how sweet they're becoming. Have a good old sniff. These are the little pleasures of cooking, the gifts a cook gets in return for making dinner. And attention to these details is what makes food taste wonderful. When garlic goes toasty and golden, it unleashes umami and colours the entire dish with its warm, nutty flavour. Onions can become incredibly sweet, leaking that sweetness into stews and sauces. The way you treat onions and garlic, even though the two are not usually the starring veg, determines the character of the final dish. Browning them will make the entire dish taste hearty, more appropriate for a chilly day. Lowering the heat and keeping them free of colour makes for a lighter-tasting dish, even when it features a hefty veg like parsnips or cauliflower. Rush the process, however, and your food will lack depth. Get distracted and your garlic will burn.

I hope you'll keep this in mind as you read my recipes. As I did in my first cookbook, I decided that instead of writing recipes that look invitingly short, I'd offer recipes full of the little details that make food great. So please don't mistake a recipe that looks long for a recipe that's too complex to cook.

## be fussy

Once you get to cooking, you should be particular, or – to be less charitable – fussy, about the ingredients you use. That the tastier these raw ingredients are the better your food will be should go without saying. Yet while I reckon that everyone agrees that a sweet pea is more delicious than a starchy bland one, I also reckon that each cook has her own quirky preferences. I embrace mine, which is why the recipes in this book are the way they are.

I leave the skin and spindly roots on beetroot, because they're tasty and pretty. I often blanch and peel tomatoes that I plan to cook with, sometimes even running the result through a food mill to achieve a smooth texture, without bothersome bits of seeds. I always peel the caps of portobello mushrooms, though I'm not quite sure why.

I'm particular, too, about some of the ingredients that many recipes in this book share. Here, you'll find a rundown of these staple ingredients that reflects my quirks. I hope you'll try things my way, but I know the way you cook is a reflection of who you are and everyone's different. Whether you adopt my eccentricities or not, you too should embrace your inner fuss-bucket and decide what you like and what gets you grumpy.

## ANCHOVIES

Anchovies are good friends to vegetables, adding salty umami but not necessarily fishy flavour. I prefer salt-packed whole anchovies to oil-packed fillets. You'll need to fillet them yourself, but it only takes a few extra minutes. If you must use the oil-packed kind, make sure they're top quality – I like the Ortiz brand – and that you gently wipe the oil from the fillets before you cook with them.

### Soaking and filleting salt-packed anchovies

Rinse the anchovies one at a time under cold running water, rubbing them gently between your fingers to remove the salt. Put them in a small bowl and add just enough water to cover. After about a minute – if you soak them for too long, they'll lose their umami quality – give them another quick rinse.

To fillet the anchovies, hold an anchovy under cold running water.

Use your fingers to brush away the soft, loose matter near the head and at the belly. Rub the outside to remove any remaining salt or hard bits. Keeping the anchovy under the water, gently work a fingertip along the belly to start to separate the fillets. Gently pull the fillets apart – this should be easy, especially once you get the hang of it. Drape the now boneless fillet over the edge of a bowl to drain. Take the second fillet and pinch the backbone, pull it gently out, and discard it. Put the second fillet next to the first. Do the same with the rest of the anchovies.

## GARLIC

In this book, I call for two types of garlic: standard garlic and spring garlic. By the time you buy standard garlic, the bulbs have hung in a warm, dry place for several weeks until the skins dry out and become papery. The process, known as 'curing', helps preserve the garlic. Spring garlic, however, is eaten right after it's pulled from the earth, and has a sweeter, milder flavour. During its season, I often use spring garlic in place of standard garlic, though I add a bit more since its flavour is not as strong. The standard garlic you get at farmers' markets is typically good and fresh. In many supermarkets, however, it often has a little bright green germ growing inside or even peeking out the tip of the cloves. If you're fussy like me, you'll slice garlic cloves in half lengthwise and flick this green bit out before you get to chopping or cooking. Some people say the green bit makes your food a bit bitter; I don't find it bitter, but have seen it contribute an off-putting blue-ish colour to what I'm cooking.

## HERBS

Herbs are delicate things. When you're washing and handling them, be gentle. With herbs like basil and mint, which oxidise easily, be especially careful and always chop or tear them just before you plan to use them. Because herbs are so fragile, I'm always torn about how to provide measurements for them. I hate the idea of calling for tablespoons and

cups, because thinking about someone cramming delicate herbs in a cup measure makes my bum cheeks clench. So I've opted for measurements that feel more natural to me: handfuls, small handfuls, and what I call five-finger pinches. Imagine a heap of mint leaves – a five-finger pinch means as much as you can grab with just the tips of all five fingers, as opposed to a typical pinch for which you'd grab with just your thumb and two fingers. Most of these measurements assume that you've picked the leaves from the tough stems. For parsley and coriander, however, I like to use what I call 'delicate sprigs', which are a few inches long and include thin, tender stems as well as leaves.

## TOMATOES

I'm plenty fussy about tomatoes, whether they're fresh or tinned. I often treat both to a little grooming before I cook with them.

### Peeling fresh tomatoes

In several recipes, I call for tomatoes to be peeled. Here's how to do it. Bring a large pot of water to the boil. Use a knife to cut a shallow 'X' at the bottom of each tomato. Working in batches of tomatoes of similar size, carefully plunge them in the boiling water and blanch for 20 seconds for larger tomatoes, and about 10 seconds for smaller ones. Gently transfer them to a colander and run them under cold running water. The peels will have loosened and you should be able to pull them off easily at the 'X'.

### Draining and trimming tinned tomatoes

Any recipe in this book that calls for tinned tomatoes asks that you drain and trim them. First, drain and discard the liquid they come in, which I find tastes artificially sweet and salty. Second, trim any yellowish patches, straggling skin, and the tough core from each tomato.

put a spring in your step

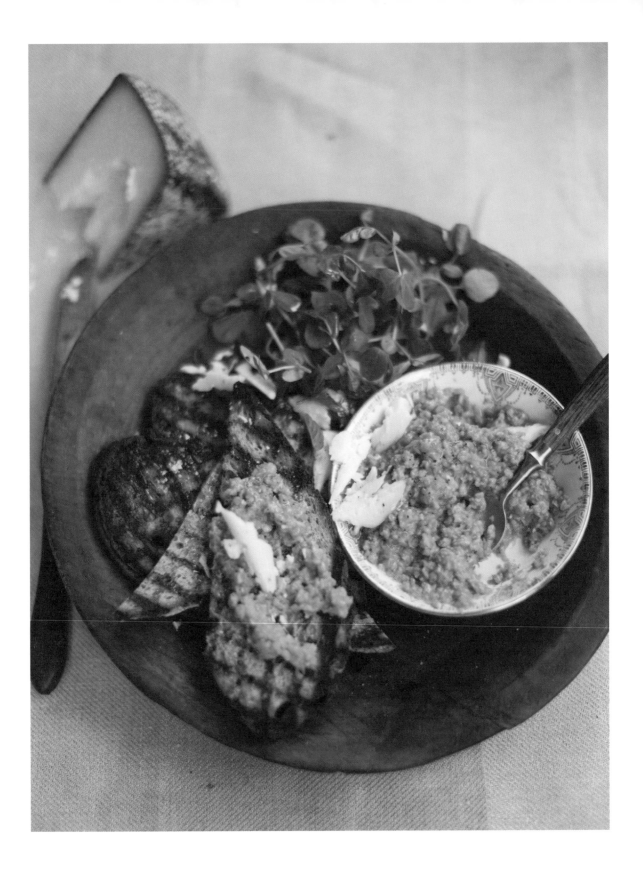

# CRUSHED SPRING PEAS WITH MINT

As a girl in England, I always loved mushy peas, whether they were made the real way – from a starchy variety of pea called marrowfat that's dried, then soaked – or dumped into a pot straight from a tin. Nowadays I prefer this mash made from fresh, sweet shelling peas – a twist on the British classic, which actually takes less work to make than its inspiration. It's wonderful spread in a thick layer on warm bread or as a dip for raw veg, like radishes, carrots, and wedges of fennel.

**makes about 300g**

300g fresh peas (from about 900g of pods)

25g aged pecorino, finely grated

1½ teaspoons Maldon or another flaky sea salt

1 small spring garlic clove or ½ small garlic clove, smashed, peeled and roughly chopped

12 medium mint leaves

3 tablespoons extra-virgin olive oil

Scant 2 tablespoons lemon juice, plus more for finishing

Combine the ingredients in a food processor and pulse to a coarse purée, about 45 seconds. Scrape the mixture into a bowl and roughly stir and smoosh a bit so it's a little creamy and a little chunky. Season to taste with more salt and lemon juice – you want it to taste sweet and bright but not acidic.

# SUGAR SNAP PEA SALAD

I admit that I'm hard on sugar snap peas. I get disappointed when they suck, of course, but I also get grumpy when they're anything less than perfect – unblemished, super sweet, and not a bit starchy. That's the curse of keeping high standards, I suppose: you're so rarely satisfied. When at last I do find perfect sugar snap peas, I make this salad. I leave them raw – only the finest snap peas can be this delightful without a dunk in boiling water – and accentuate their flavour with little more than a lemony dressing and mint. If you'd like, you could add some creamy goat's cheese in dollops or good old burrata alongside.

So long as you find the right sugar snap peas, you'll have a smashing salad. But I find that putting your knife to them adds even more excitement, a little textural variation and attractiveness. Accordingly, run the tip of your knife along the spine of some of the larger pods, open them like a book to expose the peas, and gently pull to separate the two sides of the pod. Slice others diagonally in half or thirds. Keep small ones whole.

Combine the peas and mint in a large bowl. Pour in the dressing and toss gently but well. Season to taste with more salt and lemon, if you'd like. Add the rocket to the bowl and toss gently to coat the leaves in the dressing without bruising them. Arrange it all prettily on a platter and serve straightaway.

## PREPPING SUGAR SNAP PEAS

If you wish to remove the maximum string from your sugar snap peas, try this. With one hand, hold a pea so the concave side is facing you and the stem end is facing down. With the other, use a small, sharp knife to cut just below the very tip of the pea and pull towards you, removing the string in the process. Rotate the pea so the stem end is facing up and the concave side is facing away from you. Now cut just below the tip of the pea and pull towards you, removing the string along the spine of the pea. This goes quite quickly once you get the hang of it, and you never have to worry about a stringy bit mucking up a good bite.

serves 4 as a side

450g sugar snap peas, trimmed and strings removed (see note)

A five-finger pinch of mint leaves, roughly chopped at the last minute

55ml Simple Lemon Dressing (page 238)

Maldon or another flaky sea salt

Lemon juice

A large handful of delicate, peppery rocket

# BRAISED PEAS AND LITTLE GEM LETTUCE

To me, this dish, also known as *petits pois à la française*, is a classic because the whole is so much greater than the sum of its parts. The dish isn't a vehicle for the peas or the braised lettuce to be the star; instead it's all about the magic they create together. The lettuce heads become silky and meaty, the sweet peas pop in your mouth, and all that springtime flavour infuses the broth. This dish would be delightful with duck confit, roast duck, or grilled lamb alongside, though if you're not in a meaty mood, stir in some cooked barley and you'll have a hearty meal.

Remove and reserve the floppy outer leaves from the lettuce, discarding any blemished ones. Halve the heads lengthwise. Rinse, drain, and thinly slice the reserved outer leaves.

Heat 55ml of the olive oil in a wide heavy pot over medium-high heat until it shimmers. Add the garlic and cook, occasionally flipping and stirring the cloves, until they're golden brown, 1 to 2 minutes. Use a slotted spoon to transfer the garlic to a small bowl.

Add the lettuce heads cut sides down to the pot (don't be alarmed if they spit and pop a bit) and cook until golden brown, 1 to 2 minutes. Turn them over, add ½ teaspoon or so of salt, and cook just until they've gone translucent at the stem and wilted at the tips, about 3 minutes more. It's OK if a few leaves fall off. Transfer the halved heads to a plate. Add the sliced lettuce, along with another ½ teaspoon or so of salt, to the pot and cook just until wilted and just about all the liquid in the pot has evaporated, about 2 minutes. Transfer to a medium bowl.

Give the pot a wipe, reduce the heat to medium-low, and add the remaining 2 tablespoons of oil and the butter. When the butter froths, add the onions and the cooked garlic along with 1 teaspoon of salt, have a stir, and cover the pot. Cook, stirring occasionally to make sure everything's happy, until the onions are soft and creamy but not

serves 6 as a side

3 heads Little Gem lettuce (about 450g), stems trimmed of brown but kept intact

55ml plus 2 tablespoons extra-virgin olive oil, plus a glug for finishing

6 medium spring garlic cloves or 3 medium garlic cloves, peeled and halved lengthwise

About 1 tablespoon Maldon or another flaky sea salt

1 tablespoon unsalted butter

450g young onions (see 'Young Onions', page 49) or Spanish onions, halved lengthwise and cut crosswise into 0.5cm-thick slices

110ml dry white wine, such as Sauvignon Blanc

300g shelled fresh peas (from about 900g of pods)

350ml Simple Chicken Stock (page 245)

A five-finger pinch of mint leaves, roughly chopped at the last minute coloured, about 20 minutes. Increase the heat to high, pour in the wine, and boil until it's nearly all evaporated, about 5 minutes.

Add the peas and return the cooked sliced lettuce to the pot, stir well, then return the lettuce head halves, cut sides up, to the pot along with the stock and 1 teaspoon of salt. Bring the stock to a boil, then reduce the heat to maintain a steady simmer, prodding the lettuce heads and peas a bit so they're nearly submerged. Cook just until the peas are soft but still pop in your mouth and the flavours marry, about 15 minutes, depending on the size of the peas.

Add the mint and a healthy glug of olive oil and have a stir. Add salt to taste. I like to let it cool a bit before I dig in.

# RAMPS WITH FRIED EGGS

As simple a dish as I can imagine, this heap of sweet, garlicky ramps, bright from lemon and chilli, is something I'd eat every day – if only those stubborn ramps didn't have such a short season. Yet that's part of their magic, isn't it? You can't always have them.

I like to eat the whole lot on toast. I like it with home fries. Sometimes I'll fry up a few strips of bacon first, until they're still a little bit floppy, then cook the ramps in the fat. The eggs make the dish all the more satisfying, though you can leave them out and serve the ramps as a side dish. Whether you use chicken or duck eggs, which are fattier and have a bit more character, make sure your oil is nice and hot so that when you crack in those eggs, the whites pop and spit and develop gorgeous crispy edges.

If you can't find ramps, new season leaf garlic makes a good substitute.

Halve any ramp bulbs thicker than a medium garlic clove. Cut the purple stems into 2.5-cm lengths and slice the leaves crosswise into thirds.

Combine the butter and oil in a 30cm nonstick frying pan and set it over medium heat. When the butter melts, froths and gurgles, add the stems and bulbs, increase the heat to medium-high, and cook until the bulbs turn translucent, 2 to 3 minutes.

Add a generous pinch of salt to the pan and then sprinkle the leaves

**serves 4 as a main**

350g ramps, trimmed and separated into white bulbs, purple stems, and green leaves (see note opposite)

5 tablespoons unsalted butter, cut into chunks

3 tablespoons extra-virgin olive oil

Maldon or another flaky sea salt

4 large duck or chicken eggs

2 dried pequín chillies, crumbled, or pinches of red pepper flakes

½ lemon

on top of the bulbs and stems. Stir briefly and shake the pan to distribute the greens evenly and let it all sizzle away, stirring occasionally, until the bulbs have spots of golden brown, about 6 minutes more. Use a slotted spoon to transfer the ramps to a plate, leaving behind as much fat as you can.

With the pan still over medium-high heat, crack the eggs into the pan, trying your best to leave a little space between each one. Sprinkle the chillies and a generous pinch of salt over each egg. Cook until the whites have just set, about 1 minute. Spoon the ramp mixture here and there over the eggs but not over the yolks.

Cover the pan, turn off the heat, and let sit until the eggs are cooked to your liking, 1 to 2 minutes for nice runny yolks. Season with salt to taste and squeeze on just enough lemon juice to add brightness, not acidity. Eat straightaway.

*Note: When they first appear in markets, ramp bulbs are so sweet and slender that you can add them all at once with the stems and leaves, though here I have you start the bulbs and stems a couple of minutes early, in case they're a bit starchy, which can happen further into the season.*

# POT-ROASTED ARTICHOKES
## WITH WHITE WINE AND CAPERS

One of the reasons I go giddy about springtime is artichokes, particularly the small ones with tips closed tightly, like a flower at night. Some home cooks are reluctant to fill their totes with artichokes, as they'll need to be turned – the barbed leaves plucked off and the other inedible bits trimmed away. I quite like the process. It's meditative and satisfying once you get the hang of it. In this dish, the fleshy artichokes get browned and crispy tops and look like strange, beautiful roses. The acidity in the white wine cuts through the rich, dense veg and, along with the salty pops from the capers, highlights the artichokes' unique herbaceousness.

Heat the oil in a heavy pot (wide enough to hold the artichokes with room to spare) over medium-high heat until it just begins to smoke. Stand the artichokes cut sides down in the oil, wait a minute, then reduce the heat to medium-low, sprinkle in the garlic and salt, and cook, without stirring, just until the garlic turns golden and smells toasty, about 3 minutes.

Slowly pour in the wine, cover the pot, and cook, without stirring, at a vigorous simmer until you can insert a sharp knife into the thick artichoke bottoms with barely any resistance, about 25 minutes. Five minutes or so before they're fully tender, remove the lid and scatter on the capers.

Raise the heat to medium-high, and bring the liquid to a boil. Cook until all the wine has evaporated (the bubbling sound will become a sizzle), about 3 minutes. Add the mint and parsley and keep cooking the artichokes in the oil (it's OK if a few of them tip over), until the cut sides of the artichokes are deep golden brown, 3 to 5 minutes. Lower the heat if necessary to prevent the artichokes from getting too dark.

Arrange the artichokes prettily on a plate, and scoop the capers, oil, and slightly crispy herbs over top. Serve straightaway or at room temperature.

serves 4 to 6 as a side

55ml extra-virgin olive oil

1.5kg baby artichokes (about 18), turned (see 'Turning Artichokes', page 32)

2 medium garlic cloves, thinly sliced

1½ teaspoons Maldon or another flaky sea salt

330ml dry white wine, such as Sauvignon Blanc

1 heaped tablespoon drained capers

A five-finger pinch of mint leaves, torn at the last minute

A pinch of delicate flat-leaf parsley sprigs

## TURNING ARTICHOKES

I suppose some people might find it a bother, but I quite like turning artichokes. It's like an advanced version of shelling peas – similarly meditative and even a bit fun. Choosing artichokes whose leaves don't move much when you pinch the tops will make your life a bit easier, because typically they have smaller chokes or sometimes none at all.

Fill a big bowl with water and squeeze in the juice of a lemon. Working with one artichoke at a time, pluck off and discard the green leaves until only the soft yellowish leaves are left. Cut off about 1cm of the stem. Use a peeler or small knife to trim away the tough green stuff at the base of the artichoke. Take a peek at the cut end of the stem. You'll see a pale green circle surrounded by a darker border. Peel the stem, getting as close as you can to the pale green centre. Drop the artichoke into the lemony water (to prevent discolouration). Repeat with the remaining artichokes.

Cut about 2.5cm from the tip of each artichoke, then use a small spoon to scoop out and discard the feathery choke. Gently squeeze each artichoke over the bowl as you go, and set them cut sides down on kitchen paper to drain for about 5 minutes.

*a girl and her greens*

# BOILED ASPARAGUS WITH RAMP BÉARNAISE SAUCE

Sometimes what seems like the least exciting way to cook a vegetable is the most lovely. I adore roasted and grilled asparagus, with those tempting golden-brown spots. Still, my favourite way to eat asparagus is boiled. That's when it feels the most elegant in the mouth, fat and juicy and clean when you bite it.

The stalks require little more than a drizzle of nice olive oil and perhaps a spritz of lemon, but an even more thrilling accompaniment is a rich, bright béarnaise served alongside. It's the sexiest thing, a béarnaise. I must've made this tart, rich French sauce, a sort of hot mayonnaise made with butter instead of oil, a thousand times when I worked under Rowley Leigh at the London restaurant Kensington Place. I don't think I ever got tired of dipping vegetables in it or drizzling it over grilled fish or steak. In early spring, when ramps join bunches of asparagus at farmers' markets, I swap the typical shallots for ramp bulbs and finish the sauce with ramp leaves instead of the more classic tarragon.

You can make béarnaise a few hours in advance, so long as you keep it somewhere warm. If you keep it somewhere too hot or chilly, it could split. To fix split béarnaise, add 1 teaspoon of warm water to a bowl, then add the béarnaise bit by bit, starting with a few drops and upping the amount as you go, whisking furiously with each addition.

## make the béarnaise

Combine the vinegar and the ramp bulbs and stems in a small saucepan. Bring the liquid to a gentle simmer over medium-low heat and cook, swirling occasionally, until the vinegar has fully evaporated, 5 to 8 minutes. Let the mixture cool slightly.

Fill a small pot with a couple of centimetres of water and bring the water to a boil. Grab a heatproof mixing bowl that will fit in the pot without touching the water. Combine the ramp mixture, egg yolks, and the tablespoon of hot water in the bowl and whisk well. Set the

serves 4 as a side

### FOR THE BÉARNAISE

110ml Champagne vinegar or white wine vinegar

Scant 225g ramps, trimmed, green leaves separated, and everything thinly sliced (about 75g bulbs and stems and 150g leaves)

2 large egg yolks

1 tablespoon hot water, plus more if necessary

225g Clarified Butter (page 37), warm

1 teaspoon Maldon or another flaky sea salt, or more to taste

### FOR THE ASPARAGUS

Sea salt

450g asparagus (spears as thick as an index finger), woody bottoms snapped off bowl in the pot and whisk constantly, scraping the sides of the bowl as you do and lifting the bowl from the pot every 15 seconds or so. You want to cook the yolks as gently as possible. Keep at it just until the mixture has thickened to the texture of loose mayonnaise, about 2 minutes.

Remove the bowl from the pot and wrap a damp kitchen towel around the base of the bowl to steady it. Drizzle in the clarified butter in a very slow, steady stream, whisking constantly. (If after you've added half the butter, the mixture looks really thick and shiny, whisk in another tablespoon of hot water before you add the rest of the butter.) Stir in the salt and ramp leaves, taste, and season with salt to taste.

Set the béarnaise aside in a warm place.

### make the asparagus

Bring a medium pot of water to a boil over high heat and season it generously with salt until it's a little less salty than the sea.

Add the asparagus and cook just until the asparagus is cooked through but still snappy and juicy (the spears should give slightly when you give them a gentle squeeze), 2 to 3 minutes. Use tongs or a spider to gently remove the asparagus. Drain it well, pat it dry, and arrange it on a platter. Serve the béarnaise in a bowl alongside for dipping or drizzle it prettily over the top.

# CLARIFIED BUTTER

When I plan to make béarnaise, hollandaise, and many other emulsified French sauces, my first step is to clarify butter, or melt the butter and cook it slowly so the milk solids rise to the surface to be skimmed off, leaving behind only the glass-clear yellow fat. Using this instead of regular melted butter is essential for achieving a sauce of the proper texture and also one that won't readily split on you. Even if you're not planning to make my ramp béarnaise (page 35), you should still give clarifying butter a go. For one, it's good fun to have an excuse to melt a big old hunk of butter, taking plenty of sniffs as it bubbles away. Clarified butter also makes a great cooking fat, since it won't burn at high temperatures like regular butter will.

**makes about 675g**

675g unsalted butter,
cut into about 4cm pieces

Put the butter in a medium saucepan and set it over medium-low heat. Let it melt completely, without stirring, until it begins to bubble, then have a gentle stir. Let the butter bubble steadily, without stirring, lowering the heat if you spot any browning around the edges. Some of the whitish milk solids will rise to the surface, some will cook off, and some will settle at the bottom of the pan. Cook until the yellow liquid is nearly transparent (you'll want to push the white solids on the surface aside to have a good look at the liquid), 10 to 12 minutes.

Use a spoon to gently skim the white stuff from the surface. You should be left with transparent golden fat with some opaque milk solids below. Slowly pour the yellow liquid butter into a container, leaving any remaining milk solids behind in the pan.

The clarified butter keeps in an airtight container for up to a month in the refrigerator.

# SPRING EGG DROP SOUP

I hate muddling through a long winter only to suffer those odd early spring months when the weather is finally warming up, but the markets don't seem to have noticed. Spring produce takes a while to shake off the cold. So when it does, an excitable cook like me tends to go overboard. I pop to the market to grab a bunch of asparagus and return weighed down by bags and bags of spring goodies. I want to use them all without cooking a dozen different dishes. So I make a nice soup, one flaunting a last-minute drizzle of eggs beaten with a little Parmesan so they set in silky, fatty strands. A variety of veg is fantastic here, but feel free to use just asparagus or just peas, if that's what you've got or what you like.

Heat the oil in a wide heavy pot over medium heat until it shimmers. Add the carrots first, then the onion, garlic, and 2 teaspoons of the salt. Cover and cook, stirring only after 5 minutes have passed and occasionally thereafter, until the onions are soft and creamy but not coloured, about 25 minutes.

Uncover, add all but 1 tablespoon of the chicken stock, increase the heat to high, and bring the stock to a vigorous simmer. Add the asparagus and both kinds of peas and cook just until they're tender with a slight crunch, about 3 minutes.

Meanwhile, beat the eggs with the Parmesan, a pinch of salt, and the remaining tablespoon of stock.

When the green vegetables are ready, reduce the heat to low, stir in the herbs, then drizzle the egg mixture here and there over the soup. Have one very gentle stir, wait a minute or two until the egg sets, then take the pot off the heat. Season to taste with salt (be judicious, or else you will obscure the flavour of the vegetables), then squeeze in just enough lemon to add brightness, not acidity. Let the soup cool slightly before you dig in.

serves 4

55ml extra-virgin olive oil

225g young carrots, topped, tailed, peeled and cut into 1-cm irregularly shaped pieces

230g chopped (1-cm pieces) bulbous spring onions

3 slim or 1 bulbous spring garlic head(s), roots and tops trimmed, tough layers removed, thinly sliced

2 teaspoons plus a pinch Maldon or another flaky sea salt

900ml Simple Chicken Stock (page 245)

225g asparagus, woody bottoms snapped off, cut on the diagonal into 1-cm pieces

110g sugar snap peas, trimmed, strings removed, and cut on the diagonal into 0.5-cm pieces

100g shelled fresh peas (from about 300g of pods)

2 large eggs

2 tablespoons finely grated Parmesan cheese

A five-finger pinch of mint leaves, roughly chopped at the last minute

A five-finger pinch of basil leaves, roughly chopped at the last minute

½ lemon

# WATERCRESS SOUP
# WITH SPRING GARLIC

The watercress I dream about comes from Dave Harris at Max Creek Hatchery, in Delaware County, New York. 'Hatchery'? you might wonder. Yes, Dave deals mainly in trout, fresh and smoked, but he also sells perfectly peppery, bitter watercress that grows wild by the water. He keeps sheep, too, that like to chomp on it while they're grazing. Sheep eat everything, those little buggers. This soup features the sophisticated flavour of watercress balanced by the sweetness of slowly cooked onion and spring garlic. The soup's silky body comes from potatoes, rinsed to wash away some of their starch, and, if I'm being honest, plenty of tasty fat. Fortunately, watercress is one of those vegetables whose strong flavour lets you know you're eating something good for you. I like to think that's all that matters. Add a spoonful of smoked trout roe for a special treat.

The soup will go from garden green to drab olive if you don't serve it straightaway. If you'd like to make the soup the night before but retain its bright green colour, make an ice-water bath in a bowl large enough to hold another bowl and set the second large bowl in the bath. Once the soup is done, pour it in the bowl and stir until it's cold. Transfer it to an airtight container and keep it in the fridge for up to a day.

Trim away the roots and cut off and discard the dark green tops of the spring garlic. Peel off the outermost layer from the stalks and bulbs. If your knife slides easily through the stalk about 10cm up from the bulb, thinly slice it and set aside. If not, save it to use as an aromatic in stock or sauce. Halve the bulbs lengthwise and if necessary remove any tough layers. Thinly slice the bulb, discarding anything you come across with which your knife struggles.

Melt the butter in a medium pot over medium-low heat, then add the garlic, onion, and 1 tablespoon of the salt and have a stir. Cover the pot and cook, stirring occasionally and reducing the heat if the onion threatens to colour, until the onion is very soft, creamy and sweet, about 30 minutes.

serves 4 to 6

2 spring garlic heads, with stalks attached if possible (see 'Spring Garlic', opposite)

110g plus 2 tablespoons unsalted butter

1 large Spanish onion (about 450g), halved lengthwise and thinly sliced

2½ tablespoons plus a pinch Maldon or another flaky sea salt

450g russet (baking) potatoes, peeled, cut into 1-cm pieces, rinsed and drained well

450ml whole milk

450g mature watercress (not baby), bottom 2.5cm of stems trimmed, thick stems thinly sliced, the rest left whole

A small handful of delicate chervil sprigs, optional

110ml plus 1 teaspoon extra-virgin olive oil

120g crème fraîche

½ teaspoon black peppercorns, toasted in a small pan until aromatic, then coarsely crushed

Add the potatoes, milk, the remaining 1½ tablespoons of salt, and 450ml of water. Cover the pot, increase the heat to medium, and bring the liquid to a vigorous simmer. Uncover, lower the heat if necessary to maintain a gentle simmer, and cook until the potatoes are fully tender, about 15 minutes.

Add the watercress and chervil (if you're using it), let it wilt slightly, and gently stir to submerge the greens in the liquid. Bring the mixture back to a simmer, pour in 110ml of the oil, then remove the pot from the heat.

Pour the soup into a large mixing bowl. Working in batches, blend the soup (be careful when blending hot liquids) until very smooth, adding each batch back to the pot. (Whenever I make this at one of my restaurants, I use a high-power blender, such as a Vita-Prep, to get the soup especially smooth and fully bright green rather than green-flecked.)

Keep the soup warm in the pot and season to taste with salt. Combine the crème fraîche and crushed peppercorns in a small bowl with the remaining 1 teaspoon of olive oil and a pinch of salt and stir well.

Divide the soup among bowls, top with the crème fraîche mixture and serve straightaway.

## SPRING GARLIC

At farmers' markets, you see spring garlic in different sizes. For this recipe, try to find bulbous heads that are close in size to a head of standard garlic. Sometimes, especially in early spring, the spring garlic on offer might have slim heads, about the size of spring onion bottoms. These are just fine, though you'll want to use 6 or so, including the tender parts of the stalks. Even on the larger bulbs of spring garlic, there's a chance that the bottom 10cm or so of stalk will also be tender enough to use in this recipe.

# ASPARAGUS QUICHES WITH MINT

I'm afraid that quiche has gone out of fashion, hasn't it? I think I know why. When I was growing up, I ate some truly horrible ones, both home-cooked and shop-bought, packed with what seemed like a refrigerator's worth of odds and ends suspended in overcooked egg. The only fun I'd have eating them was squidging the filling through my teeth. But as with most foods we think we don't like, a truly excellent specimen can change our minds in a bite. My hope is that this quiche does just that with a delicate, flaky crust and an eggy filling that's fluffy enough to banish those bad memories for ever.

You *could* eat quiche piping hot from the oven, of course, but I prefer it once it's cooled a bit or at room temperature. Fresh from the oven, quiche tastes mostly of crust. Only when it cools does it all balance out, the crust stepping back a few paces and the egginess and filling marching forward to say hello.

Quiche makes a great vehicle for whatever vegetables are in season and a fun way to impress when you have a crowd over for lunch. Little quiches are really cute, but feel free to make one larger quiche, if you fancy. A 28-cm tart tin will do it, though you will wind up with some extra dough.

## make the dough

Combine the flour, sugar, sea salt and baking powder in a food processor and pulse several times to mix them well. Add the butter and pulse until the mixture has the texture of fine breadcrumbs. A few pebble-size pieces of butter here and there is just fine.

Transfer the mixture to a bowl, pour in the crème fraîche and water, and use your fingertips to toss and gently smoosh the mixture just until it comes together as a dry, slightly crumbly dough. Don't overwork it and don't let it warm up too much. Cover the bowl and keep it in the fridge for 15 to 30 minutes.

Line your work surface and a baking sheet with baking parchment. Turn the dough onto the work surface and roll it out to an even

**makes twelve 8cm quiches**

SPECIAL EQUIPMENT

Twelve 8-cm wide, 2.5-cm deep ring moulds or tartlet tins

FOR THE DOUGH

375g plain flour

1 teaspoon sugar

½ teaspoon sea salt

¼ teaspoon baking powder

110g unsalted butter, well chilled and cut into 1-cm pieces

60g crème fraîche

55ml very cold water

FOR THE FILLING

Sea salt

450g asparagus (spears as thick as an index finger), woody bottoms snapped off, stalks cut into 0.5-cm pieces, tips left whole

3 tablespoons unsalted butter, cut into several chunks

115g finely diced Spanish onion (about 1 small)

0.5cm thickness, dusting the dough with flour if the rolling pin sticks to it. Trace an inverted bowl with the tip of your knife to cut out twelve 11-cm rounds. Work swiftly to line each ring mould with a dough round, pressing the sides and bottoms gently. Put them on the baking sheet, cover them with clingfilm, and refrigerate for at least 4 hours or overnight.

## bake the shells
Position a rack in the centre of the oven and preheat to 160°C/gas 3.

Cut baking parchment into twelve 12.5-cm squares. Crumple each square into a ball, wet the ball under running water, squeeze out all the water and flatten them out again. (This makes them more malleable.) Just before you're ready to bake the shells (not sooner), take them from the fridge. (They must be nice and cold when you pop them in the oven, or else your quiches will be greasy.) Use one square of baking parchment to line each shell and fill each one almost to the brim with dried beans or raw rice. (You can save the rice or beans to use the next time you bake.) Put the shells back in the fridge for about 15 minutes.

Bake, rotating the baking sheet once, just until the dough is no longer raw but not yet coloured at all, 20 to 25 minutes. Remove the beans or rice and parchment squares. Gently prick the bottom and sides of the dough with a fork, which will prevent it from puffing up as it bakes. Return to the oven and bake until the shells are evenly light golden brown and the edges have pulled away from the sides of the pans, 25 to 30 minutes. Let the shells cool completely before you fill them. Leave the oven on.

## make the filling and assemble the quiche
Bring a medium pot of water to a boil and salt it generously until it's slightly less salty than the sea. Cook the asparagus stalks in the water just until they've lost their raw crunch, 1 to 1½ minutes, using

1 small bulb spring garlic, tough outer layer removed, bulb thinly sliced and then roughly chopped, or 1 tablespoon thinly sliced regular garlic

¼ teaspoon Maldon or another flaky sea salt

2 large eggs plus 2 large egg yolks

180g double cream

165ml whole milk

8 mint leaves, thinly sliced at the last minute

**45**

a spider to transfer them to a colander to drain. Do the same with the tips, keeping them separate from the stalks.

Melt the butter in a medium cast-iron frying pan over medium-low heat until frothy. Add the onion, garlic, and Maldon salt and cook, stirring now and again, until the onion is soft and just barely browned at the edges, about 12 minutes. Remove the pan from the heat.

Combine the whole eggs and egg yolks in a large bowl and whisk briefly. Combine the cream and milk in a small pot, set it over medium-high heat, and cook just until it reaches a strong simmer. Immediately remove it from the heat, then very gradually pour it into the bowl with the eggs, whisking as you pour. Stir in 2 teaspoons of sea salt. Let the egg mixture, onion mixture and asparagus come to room temperature.

Divide the onion mixture among the shells, spreading slightly to form a layer. Spoon in the asparagus stalks (about 2 generous tablespoons per shell). Whisk the egg mixture, then ladle in enough of it to come up to about 0.5cm from the rim. Add the asparagus tips (two or three per quiche) and the mint. Pull the oven rack forward and carefully transfer the tray to the rack, then top off each quiche with a little more egg mixture. (This way the quiches won't spill as you transport them to the oven.)

Bake the quiches, rotating the baking sheet once, just until the egg mixture has set, 20 to 25 minutes. It should no longer be liquidy, but should still be soft and moist to the touch.

Remove the moulds (or, if using tartlet tins, let the quiches cool slightly before carefully removing the quiches) and let the quiches cool slightly or to room temperature before you dig in.

# ROASTED YOUNG ONIONS WITH SAGE PESTO

My knees go a bit wobbly when I pull these onions out of the oven, because I know they've given up every last bit of bite and become wonderfully creamy. They taste so sweet, you'll have a hard time convincing people that all you did was roast them with salt and olive oil. No embellishment is necessary, but salty, woodsy sage pesto sure makes a nice one.

Position a rack in the centre of the oven and preheat to 180°C/gas 4.

Cut off the onion greens, leaving just 1cm or so above the bulb. Peel off the thin, leathery outer layer of each onion and trim off the spidery roots, but make sure to leave the little nub intact (that is, the tough flat part the roots protrude from). This will keep the onions from falling apart as they cook. Halve each onion lengthwise and sprinkle the cut sides with a few healthy pinches of salt.

Find an ovenproof cast-iron frying pan or heavy enamelled baking dish wide enough to hold the onion halves in a single layer with a little room to spare. Add 3 tablespoons of the oil to the pan and set it over high heat until the oil just begins to smoke. Lower the heat to medium, carefully add the onions cut sides down and cook, using tongs to peek under the onions occasionally, until you see spots of golden brown, 5 to 8 minutes.

Pop the pan in the oven and cook until the cut sides are an even deeper golden brown but have no black spots, 20 to 25 minutes. Carefully turn the onions over with tongs and raise the oven temperature to 220°C/gas 7. Continue cooking until the onions are very soft but not falling apart, 10 to 15 minutes more.

Meanwhile, put the sage in a small food processor with the garlic, pine nuts, Parmesan and 1 teaspoon of salt, and pulse several times. Add the remaining 110ml of oil to the mixture and process full-on,

serves 4 to 6 as a side

6 young onions (the size of tennis balls), yellow, red, or a combination (see 'Young Onions', opposite)

Maldon or another flaky sea salt

110ml plus 3 tablespoons extra-virgin olive oil

A big handful of sage leaves

1 small garlic clove, roughly chopped

3 tablespoons pine nuts

25g Parmesan cheese, finely grated

stopping to scrape down the sides and stir gently if necessary, until the mixture is well combined but still chunky.

Arrange the onions prettily on a plate. Spoon some pesto, as much as you like, here and there on top of the onions. (Reserve the remaining pesto for another day.) Eat straightaway.

## YOUNG ONIONS

At farmers' markets in the spring, you'll spot piles of onions with their greens attached. The onion bulbs will either be slim, like those of scallions, or bulbous. I think of the former as spring onions. I think of the latter, which are what you want for this recipe, as young onions, because their bulbs are big enough to become sweet and creamy in the oven but haven't yet been left to cure and develop the papery skins of mature onions. I'm reluctant to say that you can substitute mature red onions, which have a sharper bite, because the result won't be quite as sweet and delicious. Reluctant, but not opposed.

*put a spring in your step* **49**

the
humble potato

# BOILED POTATOES
# WITH BUTTER AND MINT

I never get bored with potatoes. They're one of those quietly wonderful vegetables. The potato isn't flashy. It doesn't advertise with bright colours like tomatoes or carrots. It's not a fleeting beauty like ramps. It doesn't have the big, sweet flavour of corn or peas. The potato, rather, is comforting and always there for you. The potato is like a good mate you've known for ever.

I discovered my affection for the potato in primary school. Me and my little friends would storm the cafeteria at lunch. Most of the food was rubbish, except the buttery boiled potatoes, which I'd eat by the pile. This is my grown-up version. It's barely more complicated – the mint adds brightness and the lemon cuts through the starch and fat – but a lot more moreish. For you Yanks, moreish just means that each bite makes you want to eat more of it.

serves 4 as a side

450g small potatoes all, about the same size

1 tablespoon Maldon or another flaky sea salt

50g unsalted butter, cut into several pieces

1 small garlic clove, finely grated

A five-finger pinch of mint leaves, roughly torn at the last minute

½ lemon

Coarsely ground black pepper

Put the potatoes and the salt in a medium straight-sided pan or small, shallow pot, add enough water to cover the potatoes by 1cm or so, and set the pot over high heat. Bring the water to a boil, reduce the heat to maintain a vigorous simmer, and cook until fully tender and creamy inside, about 20 minutes. Reserving 55ml of the cooking liquid, drain the potatoes (gently so they don't break) and return them to the pot.

Add the butter, garlic and reserved cooking liquid to the pot and set it over medium-high heat. Let the butter melt and the liquid bubble until the liquid looks milky, 1 to 2 minutes. Cook at a vigorous simmer, tilting the pan and swirling the liquid occasionally, until the liquid reduces to a slightly viscous glaze, about 5 minutes.

Add the mint, stir gently but well, and take the pot off the heat. Squeeze on just enough lemon juice to add brightness, not acidity, and add pepper and more salt to taste. Serve straightaway.

You'll find many recipes for potatoes in this book. But my love for the lowly potato began at my school cafeteria with this simple preparation: boiled and buttered. Making them at home requires no recipe, just a bit of care and attention.

First, you must find potatoes with some character. In England, I'd go mad for the Jersey Royal. This is a springtime potato grown in the soil of Jersey, the French-speaking island in the English Channel. Farmers there use seaweed as fertiliser, just one of the reasons that these are extra special potatoes: earthy, sweet and creamy. In the States, any new potatoes – those dug before they've reached maturity and all the sugars have turned to starch – hit the spot. They're so good that your only job as a cook is not to muck them up.

So long as you give the potatoes a good rinse and gentle rub with your fingers, you can leave the thin skins on. If some of the potatoes are larger than others, cut them into similarly sized pieces, so they'll all be done at the same time. Pop them into a pot, add enough water to cover them by a couple of centimetres and add plenty of salt, because starchy things like potatoes don't absorb salt easily. You should add enough salt so that when it dissolves the water will taste a little less salty than the sea does.

Bring the water to a boil, then reduce the heat to maintain a steady simmer – the larger the potatoes, the more gentle the simmer should be to ensure even cooking – and cook until they're tender and creamy. To tell when they're done, here's a trick I learned: stick a small sharp knife into one of the potatoes, then lift the knife – if the potato comes up with the knife then slides right off by itself, the potatoes are done. Just don't get poke happy or the potatoes will get waterlogged. Drain the potatoes carefully in a colander, then let them sit for a few minutes so some water escapes as steam. While they're still hot, put them in a bowl and toss them with plenty of butter, cut into pieces, until it melts. Top with coarsely ground black pepper and a nice sprinkling of salt, if you'd like.

# SALT-CRUSTED POTATOES WITH HERBED VINEGAR

serves 4 to 6 as a side

Here's a nice, unusual way to cook my old pal the potato. For the typical boiled potatoes, I'd simmer them gently in salty water. For this preparation, the bubbles are furious. In fact, you're meant to boil the water not just until the potatoes are cooked but until it evaporates altogether. (While I do it, I like to think of a salt lake drying out to become a salt flat.) The salt left behind coats each potato to form a toasty crust that reminds me of a perfect baked potato with an especially salty jacket. Then all you do is spoon on a mixture of vinegar and fresh herbs. Just don't serve the potatoes in a bowl or stir them, or you'll lose the crust and the whole dish will get too salty.

Put the potatoes in a medium pot where they'll fit snugly in one layer and add enough cold water to just barely cover them. Add the salt and bring the water to a boil over high heat. Boil until the potatoes are tender and the water has completely evaporated, giving the pan an occasional shake once the water's almost all gone, 30 to 40 minutes. Keep cooking, and shaking, until the potatoes are coated with a layer of salt and the bottom of the pot has begun to brown (don't fret; it'll scrub off easily later), about 3 minutes more. Take the pot off the heat and let the potatoes cool slightly.

If any potatoes have a very thick layer of salt, gently rub them with a kitchen towel to knock a bit off. Halve the potatoes the long way and arrange them cut sides up on a large platter or plate. Whisk together the oil and vinegar in a small bowl until the mixture looks creamy. Toss the herbs together, coarsely chop them, and stir them into the vinegar mixture. Spoon the mixture over the potatoes, sprinkle on as much pepper as you'd like and serve straightaway.

900g golf-ball-size waxy potatoes

3 tablespoons Maldon or another flaky sea salt

55ml extra-virgin olive oil

2 tablespoons red wine vinegar or sherry vinegar

A five-finger pinch of delicate flat-leaf parsley sprigs

6 or so large basil leaves

10 or so large mint leaves

Coarsely ground black pepper

# HASSELBACK POTATOES WITH LARDO AND ROSEMARY

Rumour has it that these potatoes were invented at a restaurant in Stockholm called Hasselbacken. Whoever did come up with them is clever, indeed. The technique involves making parallel slits the length of the potato, cutting into but not completely through each spud and then roasting them, so they expand like an accordion and get extra crispy as they cook. The result is potatoes you want to eat with your hands.

When I make this dish, I like to tuck a sliver of lardo, Italian cured fatback, in some of those slits. As the potatoes cook, the lardo melts, basting the potatoes and going all crispy itself. Tucking in the lardo can be fiddly and take a while. (You might call it a bit of a *hassle,* if you don't mind bad puns.) Keep at it. Remember that lardo cooperates better when it's well chilled and that these are special-occasion potatoes that are worth the effort. But if you get really grumpy, stick to two or three pieces of lardo per potato rather than four or five.

Position a rack in the centre of the oven and preheat to 200°C/gas 6.

Working with one potato at a time, cut through the potato crosswise every 0.5 to 0.25cm as though you were cutting the potato into slices but stopping about 0.5cm before you reach the bottom. (I like to insert a thin skewer or cake tester lengthwise through the potato and stop cutting when I hit the skewer.) Repeat with the remaining potatoes. Rinse the potatoes well under water, carefully pulling open the slits to expose the flesh to the water, then drain well.

Cut the lardo slices crosswise into pieces about as long as the width of each potato. Tuck the pieces of lardo inside some of the slits (2 to 5 pieces per potato, depending on your mood), being careful not to break the potatoes. It's nice if a portion of each piece of lardo is sticking out. You might want to keep half the lardo in the fridge as you work, so it stays firm and is therefore easier to work with.

serves 4 to 6 as a side

900g small, non-waxy potatoes (about 16, each about the size and shape of an egg)

50g thinly sliced lardo, well chilled

55ml extra-virgin olive oil

Maldon or another flaky sea salt

3 rosemary sprigs

Arrange the potatoes lardo side up in a heavy enamelled baking dish large enough to fit them with a little space between each one. Drizzle on the oil, making sure each potato gets some, and sprinkle a healthy pinch of salt over each one. Bake the potatoes, rotating the dish occasionally, until the visible lardo turns golden brown and crisp and the slits begin to open up a bit, about 45 minutes.

Carefully tip the dish so the fat pools, then use a spoon to baste each potato. Keep cooking, basting once more, until the potato flesh is creamy, about 30 minutes more.

Baste once more, then flip the potatoes and cook until the bottoms look good and crispy, about 15 minutes.

Add the rosemary to the baking dish, resting some of the potatoes on and others near the sprigs so they pick up some of the rosemary's flavour, and cook for another 5 minutes or so. Baste once more, season with salt to taste, then transfer the potatoes to a plate, drizzling a little of the flavourful fat over top, if you wish. Serve straightaway.

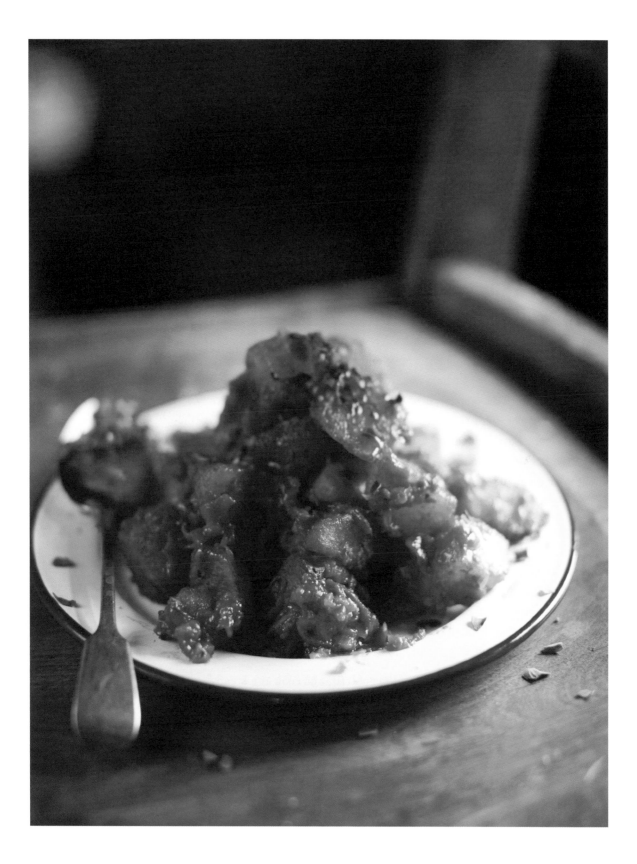

# PATATAS BRAVAS

There are two main versions of *patatas bravas*, the common Spanish tapas dish that features crispy fried potatoes: one that's drizzled with aioli and another that's topped with sweet, smoky tomato sauce. I prefer the second – to me, the first is just chips and mayonnaise, not that there's anything wrong with chips with mayonnaise – especially when the potatoes are tossed in the sauce and eaten straightaway, before they lose their crunch. They make an impressive side dish all by themselves, though fried eggs on top turn them into a proper meal for four.

### make the sauce

Peel the skin from the peppers using a vegetable peeler and a gentle sawing motion. Cut the peppers into 2.5-cm pieces. Heat 55ml of the oil in a wide, heavy medium pot over high heat until it smokes lightly. Add the onion, chillies, garlic and salt. Have a stir and cook, stirring occasionally, until the onions wilt a bit, about 3 minutes. Add the peppers and paprika, but don't stir until the onions begin to brown, about 3 minutes more. Now stir and cook, stirring and scraping the bottom often, until the onions and peppers are tender, about 10 minutes. Lower the heat to medium and keep stirring and scraping until everything is very soft and sweet, 12 to 15 minutes more.

Meanwhile, core and quarter the tomatoes, put them in a large mixing bowl, and gently squeeze to release the juice and seeds. Transfer the tomatoes to a second large bowl, leaving the liquid and seeds behind, shaking the tomatoes over the first bowl so any liquid caught in the crevices spills out. Set a strainer over the bowl with the tomatoes and pour the liquid through the strainer, smooshing to make sure you extract as much liquid as you can and discarding the solids.

Add the tomatoes and their liquid to the pot, stir, and cook at a steady simmer, stirring now and then, until most of the visible liquid has evaporated, 45 minutes to 1 hour. Stir in the marjoram. Keep cooking, stirring and scraping the pot often, until the sauce starts to stick to

serves 6 to 8 as a side

SPECIAL EQUIPMENT

An electric deep-fryer (preferable) or a large, heavy pot (such as a casserole), a deep-frying thermometer, and a spider

FOR THE SAUCE

675g red peppers (about 3 medium), halved lengthwise, seeded and deribbed

55ml extra-virgin olive oil, plus a good drizzle for finishing

1 large Spanish onion (about 560g), halved and cut into 0.5-cm thick slices

Scant 100g moderately spicy fresh red chillies, halved lengthwise, stemmed and roughly chopped (including seeds)

4 medium garlic cloves, thinly sliced

2 teaspoons Maldon or another flaky sea salt

1 teaspoon sweet smoked Spanish paprika (pimentón dulce)

1.35kg tomatoes, peeled (see page 16)

the bottom of the pot and the mixture is very thick, a bit like jam, about 10 minutes more. Take the pot off the heat.

## fry the potatoes

Put the potatoes in a medium pot, pour in enough water to cover, and add enough sea salt to make the water taste good and salty. Bring the water to a boil over high heat. Lower the heat to maintain a simmer and cook until the potatoes are just tender, about 5 minutes. Drain the potatoes well in a colander, then gently shake and toss them in the colander just until the potatoes get a bit fluffy looking on the outsides. (The rough sides will get especially crispy when the potatoes are fried.) Let them sit uncovered until they've cooled to room temperature.

Meanwhile, pour at least 5cm of fat or oil into an electric deep-fryer (or into a casserole with a deep-frying thermometer clipped to the side) and heat to 150°C/300°F. Working in batches (to avoid crowding), fry the potatoes until they develop a creamy texture (they shouldn't be browned at all), about 5 minutes. As they cook, shake the frying basket or gently stir occasionally to prevent them from sticking together. Use a spider to transfer the potatoes to a bowl and give them a gentle toss so they have another chance to go fluffy.

Bring the fat or oil temperature to 180°C/350°F. Line a bowl or tray with kitchen paper. Fry the potatoes again in batches, stirring occasionally, until they're very crispy and deep golden brown on the outsides, about 15 minutes. Transfer them to the kitchen paper to drain and immediately add a light sprinkle of Maldon salt.

Just before the potatoes are done, bring the sauce to a sizzle.

The key to the next step is doing it seconds before you serve the dish, so the potatoes stay a bit crispy: add the fried potatoes to the sauce, stir briefly but well, and transfer the sauced potatoes to a plate. Add a good drizzle of olive oil and more salt if you fancy. Serve straightaway.

A small handful of marjoram leaves, roughly chopped at the last minute

FOR THE POTATOES

1.35kg waxy potatoes, peeled, cut into irregular 2.5-cm pieces and rinsed well

Sea salt

Rendered duck fat, pork fat or peanut oil for deep-frying

Maldon or another flaky sea salt

# POTATO SOUP WITH GARLIC AND PARSLEY

If I could get away with opening a restaurant that served only boiled potatoes with butter and black pepper, I just might. Of course, customers expect a bit more from a chef than boiled potatoes, however delicious they may be. This soup is my attempt at a middle ground between plain boiled and don't-try-this-at-home knotty – it's barely more complicated than its inspiration, but a bit more elegant. The magic of starch gives the soup a luxurious velvety texture, and the toasty garlic and parsley stirred in last minute give each slurp extra complexity.

### make the soup
Heat the oil in a large pot over high heat until it smokes lightly. Add the butter, onion, garlic, and salt and stir. Cover the pot and reduce the heat to medium-low. Cook, stirring now and again, until the onions are very soft and creamy but not coloured at all, about 25 minutes. If you spot any browning, reduce the heat.

Add the potatoes and stock to the pot. Cover the pot, raise the heat to high, and bring to a boil. Uncover the pot and lower the heat to maintain a steady simmer. Simmer until the potatoes are very tender, about 25 minutes.

Pour the soup into a large mixing bowl. Working in batches, blend the soup (be careful when blending hot liquids) until very smooth and silky, adding each batch back to the pot. Keep it warm over very low heat while you prepare the garnish. (The soup keeps covered in the fridge for a day or two. When you're ready to serve it, reheat it gently until it's good and hot.)

### finish the soup
Just before you serve the soup, heat the olive oil in a medium cast-iron frying pan over high heat until it smokes lightly. Add the garlic and

serves 6 to 8

FOR THE SOUP

55ml extra-virgin olive oil

2 tablespoons unsalted butter

1 medium Spanish onion (about 350g), halved lengthwise and thinly sliced

6 medium garlic cloves, thinly sliced

3 tablespoons Maldon or another flaky sea salt

1.5kg waxy potatoes, peeled, cut into 1-cm pieces and rinsed well

1.35 litres Simple Chicken Stock (page 245)

FOR FINISHING

2 tablespoons extra-virgin olive oil, plus a healthy drizzle

4 medium garlic cloves, very thinly sliced

A big handful of delicate flat-leaf parsley sprigs, very roughly chopped

Maldon or another flaky sea salt

cook, shaking and swirling the pan, until the garlic goes golden brown at the edges, 30 seconds to 1 minute. Add the parsley and a generous pinch of salt, stir, and cook until the parsley wilts and goes a bit crispy, about 1 minute.

Scrape the garlic-parsley mixture into the hot soup. Stir in a healthy drizzle of olive oil and cream, some black pepper, and salt to taste. Haul the pot to the table with a ladle and serve straightaway.

A healthy drizzle of double cream

Freshly ground black pepper

top to tail

# WHOLE POT-ROASTED CAULIFLOWER WITH TOMATOES AND ANCHOVIES

Many years ago, when I was at the River Café, I saw my mentor Rose Gray cook a head of cauliflower as if it were a hunk of meat. I watched her lift the whole thing out of the pot and slice it into slabs, like a lamb shoulder. When I got stuck in, the dish reminded me of roast dinner, with all the complex flavours and satisfying heft, except without any meat. You can use any old type of cauliflower, though I think the green variety looks especially nice with the red sauce. Even better, find Romanesco cauliflower, with its spiral florets, like a veg from another planet.

Position a rack in the centre of the oven and preheat to 230°C/gas 8.

Put the cauliflower on its side on a cutting board. Trim the base of the stem of any brown bits, if necessary. Remove the core at the bottom as though you were coring a tomato: insert a small sharp knife about 2.5cm into the base of the stem, make a circular cut to loosen the core, then pry it out and discard. The core can be tough, plus the hollow allows the heat to penetrate the head while it cooks.

Heat the oil in a heavy oven-safe pot (wide enough to hold the cauliflower with about 8cm to spare and deep enough to cover with a lid) over medium-high heat until it smokes lightly. Add the cauliflower cored side up and spend 5 minutes or so browning it, using tongs to rotate it and lowering the heat if the browned patches threaten to get too dark. Carefully turn the head over to brown the stem side slightly, about 2 minutes.

Move the cauliflower to one side of the pot (you may transfer it to a plate if your pot isn't quite wide enough, then return it to the pot once you add the tomatoes) and add the garlic, anchovies, and rosemary to the other side. Cook, stirring a bit, until the garlic is light golden

**serves 4 to 6 as a side**

1 medium head Romanesco, green or white cauliflower (about 1kg), all but imperfect stalks and leaves left on

5 tablespoons extra-virgin olive oil, plus a healthy drizzle for finishing

3 medium garlic cloves, thinly sliced

3 salt-packed whole anchovies, soaked and filleted (see page 13)

¾ teaspoon finely chopped rosemary leaves

225g drained, trimmed and coarsely chopped tinned whole tomatoes (see page 16)

55ml dry white wine, such as Sauvignon Blanc, plus several glugs

3 dried pequín chillies, crumbled, or pinches of red pepper flakes

1 teaspoon Maldon or another flaky sea salt

brown, about 30 seconds. Move the cauliflower back into the centre, then add the tomatoes, 55ml of the wine, the chillies and the salt. Spend a minute or so stirring, basting, and piling some of the solids onto the cauliflower.

Cover the pot, lower the heat if necessary to maintain a simmer, and cook for 5 minutes or so (just so the tomatoes have a chance to concentrate in flavour). Pop the pot in the oven and roast, basting occasionally, until you can stick a knife into the thickest part of the head with almost no resistance, 45 minutes to 1 hour. Your goal as it roasts is to peek under the lid every 15 minutes or so to check on the sauce. It should be liquidy but still taste punchy and intense, so add a glug of wine whenever it threatens to get too thick.

Carefully transfer the cauliflower head to a plate, cut it in half through the stem or slice it like a roast, and spoon on all the tasty stuff left in the pot. Add a healthy drizzle of olive oil and dig in.

# ROASTED CARROTS WITH CARROT-TOP PESTO AND BURRATA

If you can get your hands on burrata – a really special cheese, like delicate mozzarella with a creamy centre – then you're already most of the way towards a great dish. In the spring, I'll serve burrata with Sugar Snap Pea Salad (page 23); in high summer, I'll pair it with slices of ripe tomato, good olive oil and flaky salt. When summer fades, I crave burrata with roasted carrots, a pairing that's less common but no less worthy of your attention. The two are like good mates, each helping the other along: the sweetness of the carrots sets off the tanginess of the cheese; the cheese's tanginess makes the carrots tastes even sweeter. Pesto made from the carrot tops adds colour and salty, herbaceous wallops throughout the dish.

Position a rack in the centre of the oven and preheat to its highest temperature.

Pour 2 tablespoons of the oil into a heavy ovenproof pan big enough to hold the carrots in a single layer. Set the pan over high heat and bring the oil to a light smoke. Add the carrots, sprinkle on 1 teaspoon of the salt, and turn the carrots to coat them in the oil. Cook, turning over the carrots occasionally, until they're browned in spots, 6 to 8 minutes. Pop the pan in the oven and roast, shaking the pan occasionally, until the carrots are evenly tender, 8 to 12 minutes, depending on the size of your carrots. Let the carrots cool slightly. Halve the burrata and arrange the halves on a platter. Arrange the carrots on the platter so they're pointing this way and that. Add the pesto here and there in little dollops.

Pluck enough 5- to 8-cm delicate sprigs from the reserved carrot tops to make about 40g and toss them in a bowl with the basil. Whisk together the remaining 2 tablespoons of the oil with the

serves 4 to 6 as a side

20 small carrots (the size of index fingers), scrubbed well but not peeled, all but 1cm of the tops removed and reserved

4 tablespoons extra-virgin olive oil

1 teaspoon plus a few pinches of Maldon or another flaky sea salt

225g room-temperature burrata, drained

About 3 tablespoons Carrot-Top Pesto (page 234)

A five-finger pinch of basil leaves, torn at the last minute if large

1 tablespoon lemon juice

lemon juice and a good pinch of salt in a small bowl until the mixture looks creamy. Use a little of the lemon dressing to lightly dress the carrot-top and basil mixture, sprinkle on a little more salt and toss well. Arrange the mixture on top of the carrots and burrata. Drizzle everything with the remaining lemon dressing and serve.

# ROASTED WHOLE
# BABY TURNIPS

I can't bear to pass by baby or Tokyo turnips (also called Japanese or Harukei turnips) when I see them at the market. First off, I know that this variety gets especially sweet and juicy when cooked. But almost as important, they're very, very cute. You'd be mad to ignore the greens, of course, and not just because they make up ninety percent of the veg you hauled home, but also because when they go wilty and slightly crispy in the oven they take on an awesome, almost seaweedy flavour. This tangle of turnips and greens makes a perfect appetizer platter, perhaps alongside thinly sliced prosciutto, which you and your mates can go at with your fingers, lifting each nibble by the greens.

Position a rack in the centre of the oven and preheat to 220°C/gas 7.

Halve each turnip lengthwise, making sure each half has plenty of stems and leaves attached. Submerge the turnips (greens and all) in a large container of water, gently swishing the greens around with your hands to dislodge any grit. Next, hold the base of the greens of each turnip under running water for a few seconds, gently separating the stems to make sure no grit is hiding out. Drain very well on kitchen paper and pat dry.

Pour 3 tablespoons of the oil into a very wide, ovenproof cast-iron frying pan or enamelled baking dish big enough to hold the turnips in a single layer. Set the frying pan over medium-high heat and bring the oil to a smoke. (If using a baking dish, it should either straddle two burners or you should rotate it occasionally to make sure it gets even heat.)

Add the turnips cut sides down to the oil in one layer. This is a bit of a puzzle to solve, but it's good fun. You'll probably need to position the turnips so the greens face this way and that and some hang over the sides of the frying pan. Cook until the cut sides are light golden brown, 5 to 8 minutes. Sprinkle on the salt and half of the parsley,

serves 4 to 6 as a side

16 baby turnips (each a little smaller than a ping-pong ball), all but imperfect roots, stems and leaves left on

3 tablespoons extra-virgin olive oil, plus a healthy drizzle for finishing

2 teaspoons Maldon or another flaky sea salt

A large handful of delicate flat-leaf parsley sprigs, roughly chopped

About 1 tablespoon red wine vinegar

*top to tail*  **73**

then tuck all the turnip greens inside the frying pan or baking dish and put it in the oven.

Roast, peeking at the cut sides and fluffing up the greens occasionally, until the greens are wilted, tender, and crispy in parts and the turnips are very tender (you should be able to insert a sharp knife with no resistance), 20 to 25 minutes. As you cook, carefully turn over any turnips whose undersides threaten to get darker than golden brown.

Remove the baking dish from the oven. Sprinkle on just enough vinegar so that you can taste its flavour but not its sting and the remaining parsley. Drizzle on some olive oil and sprinkle on more salt, if you fancy. Have a gentle toss and serve straightaway.

# SWISS CHARD (LEAVES AND STEMS) WITH MARJORAM

Sometimes I'll do nothing more than boil chard and eat the silky, lemony leaves with just a drizzle of olive oil and a sprinkle of salt. When I want something a little more substantial, I take the extra step of sautéing the boiled chard in oil, adding red onion for its meatiness and garlic for its roasty complexity and the way it rounds off the sharp, acidic edge of the chard. The preparation makes a fine filling for cannelloni (page 137) or a satisfying side dish all by itself.

(page 137)

serves 4 to 6 as a side

Sea salt

900g green Swiss chard (2 or 3 bunches), stems and leaves separated

55ml extra-virgin olive oil

1 medium red onion (about 350g), finely diced

1 teaspoon Maldon or another flaky sea salt

2 medium garlic cloves, sliced

2 five-finger pinches of marjoram leaves

Bring a large pot of water to a boil and add enough sea salt so it tastes lightly salty. Add the chard leaves and cook just until they're tender and tear very easily, 1 to 2 minutes. Drain the leaves well, let them cool, lightly squeeze them to get rid of some of the water, and roughly chop them.

Heat the oil in a medium pot or casserole over high heat. When the oil shimmers, add the onion and salt, reduce the heat to medium-low, and cook at a steady sizzle, stirring occasionally, until the onion is soft and lightly browned at the edges, 12 to 15 minutes.

Meanwhile, toss the garlic and marjoram together on a cutting board, and chop them very finely until the mixture looks a bit like blue cheese. Add the garlic mixture to the onions, stir, and cook until the garlic is golden brown, about 3 minutes.

While the garlic cooks, trim off any brown bits from the chard stems and thinly slice the stems. When the garlic has browned, add the stems to the pot. Stir, cover, and cook, stirring now and then, until they're fully tender, about 12 minutes. Add the chard leaves to the pot, cover the pot again, and cook, stirring occasionally, for a few minutes just to let the flavours mingle.

Serve hot as a side dish or let cool to room temperature if you're making cannelloni.

# BOILED BEETROOT, STEMS AND GREENS

When I find beautiful bunches at the market, I use them from nose to tail – or at least from root to leaf. Beetroot greens are too often discarded. When the greens are pert and unblemished, you'd be mad to ignore them. That'd be as rash as buying a pig and tossing away its ears and feet. I even keep the beetroot skins on. If beetroot wasn't always served peeled, I think people would cook it more. Keeping the skins on spares you purply hands. The skins taste quite nice, too.

Trim the beetroot stems to about 1cm, reserving the rest of the stems and leaves. Leave the beetroot's spindly roots intact. Cut the stems from the leaves. Keep the leaves whole and cut the stems into 10cm lengths. You should have about 60g of stems and 3 large handfuls of leaves.

Pour 5cm of water into a medium pot, add the garlic and thyme, and bring the water to a boil over high heat. Season the water with sea salt so it tastes a little less salty than the sea. Add the beetroot and boil, stirring occasionally and topping off the water if the level drops below the beetroot, until the beetroot is tender but not mushy, about 40 minutes.

Use a slotted spoon to transfer the beetroot to a mixing bowl. Halve any larger beetroot through the stem, if you fancy. Add the olive oil, tarragon, shallots, Maldon salt and vinegar, and have a good stir.

Remove and discard the garlic and thyme from the water. Add about 700ml of water to the pot, let it return to the boil and add the beetroot stems. Cook, stirring occasionally, until they're tender with a slight bite, about 4 minutes. Use the slotted spoon to transfer the stems to the bowl with the beetroot.

Add the greens to the water, have a good stir and cook just until they tear easily, about 3 minutes. Drain the leaves in a colander, let

20 or so golf-ball-size baby beetroots, with healthy greens

6 medium garlic cloves, unpeeled

6 or so small thyme sprigs

Sea salt

55ml extra-virgin olive oil

A five-finger pinch of tarragon leaves, roughly chopped

1 tablespoon finely chopped shallots

2 teaspoons Maldon or another flaky sea salt

1 teaspoon good, thick balsamic vinegar

them cool to the touch and gently squeeze them to remove some of the water they've absorbed.

Give the beetroots and stems another good stir, then use your hands to pile them on a plate. Add the greens to the liquid remaining in the mixing bowl, toss well, then transfer them to the plate as well. Eat straightaway.

satisfying salads

# BITTER LEAVES WITH POMEGRANATE AND GRILLED-VEGETABLE VINAIGRETTE

Salads, to me, are about balance and surprise. Here I assemble an array of bitter leaves – some crunchy and others soft, some mild and others bracingly sharp – and toss them with sweet-sour pomegranate seeds and a fluffy grating of salty cheese. The sneaky bits of grilled vegetables in the dressing provide the occasional delight of biting into a meaty chunk of fennel or sweet onion.

I'd happily make this salad with tight round heads of standard radicchio, but to make the salad really special, I look for thrilling varieties like Castelfranco, with its looser speckled heads, or tardivo, whose narrow, sturdy leaves resemble long fingers. And because even the loveliest radicchio can go a bit limp at the market or in the fridge, I'll typically soak the leaves for about 15 minutes in icy water before making the salad.

Combine the radicchio, kale, and endive in a very large mixing bowl. Add the dressing and toss very well with your hands. Make sure you distribute the grilled bits in the dressing and give the leaves a good rub to coat them with the liquidy part of the dressing. Add the pomegranate seeds, have another gentle toss, and transfer the salad to a large shallow bowl or platter. Sprinkle on the pecorino and serve straightaway.

**serves 4 to 6 as a side**

350g radicchio (preferably a few varieties), root ends trimmed off, separated into individual leaves and torn into bite-size pieces

1 small bunch Tuscan kale (cavolo nero), thick stems removed, leaves torn into bite-size pieces

100g Belgian endive, root end trimmed off, halved crosswise, bottom half sliced, and top half separated into individual leaves

Grilled-Vegetable Vinaigrette (page 236)

50g pomegranate seeds

25g aged pecorino cheese, finely grated

# GREEK SALAD

Some of my favourite recipes are those that rely on the little things. Take this version of Greek salad. First, you choose your ingredients carefully – for instance, ripe tomatoes (taut-skinned and unblemished), of course, but also perfect cucumbers (sweet, crisp ones with character; none that are watery or full of big old seeds). Then, have a bit of fun cutting them: using a very sharp knife (this will spare you mushy, ragged-edged tomatoes), cut them into different shapes of similar size, some with sharp angles. These and a few other small details – briefly chilling the tomatoes and cucumbers and quick-pickling the onions – turn a familiar collection of ingredients into a really special salad.

Put the cucumbers and tomatoes in separate bowls and pop them in the fridge just until they're cold, about 30 minutes.

Meanwhile, put the onions in a small bowl. Add the vinegar, 2 tablespoons of the oil and a healthy pinch of salt, and mix well with your hands. Let the onions sit just until they get pickly, a few minutes.

In a separate small bowl, stir together the remaining 2 tablespoons of oil, the lemon juice, and a good pinch of salt until the mixture looks creamy. Combine the tomatoes and cucumber in one bowl, pour in the lemon dressing and toss gently but well.

Grab a large platter (or 4 to 6 plates) and make a pretty layer of cucumbers and tomatoes, so the colours and types of the vegetables are well divvied up. Give the onions one more toss, then use your hands to add them (reserving their pickly liquid) here and there over the cucumbers and tomatoes. Scatter on the olives and mint. Use your hands to crumble the feta into pieces large, medium, and small as you scatter it on top. Finally, drizzle on the liquid remaining in the onion bowl. Eat straightaway.

serves 4 to 6 as a side

350g crunchy cucumbers without big seeds (preferably a few varieties), peeled and cut into irregular 2-cm pieces

Generous 450g mixed heirloom tomatoes, halved, cored, trimmed of any pale bits and cut into irregular 2.5-cm pieces

100g cherry tomatoes, halved through the stem end if large

2 slender spring onions, green tops and root ends trimmed, bulbs cut into 0.5-cm thick rounds and separated into rings

2 tablespoons sherry or Banyuls vinegar (available at specialty shops and online)

4 tablespoons extra-virgin olive oil

Maldon or another flaky sea salt

1 tablespoon lemon juice

20 or so Niçoise olives, firmly pressed with the flat of a knife and pitted

A five-finger pinch of mint leaves

150g creamy feta cheese (preferably goat's feta)

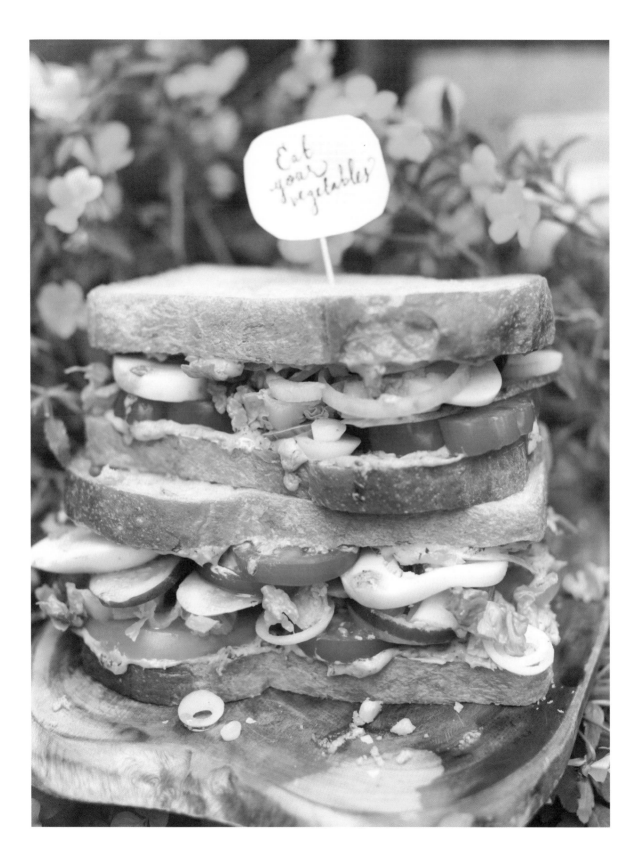

# SALAD SANDWICHES

Don't tell me you've never had a salad sandwich! When I was a girl, my family practically lived on them come summer, when it was steamy outside and the last thing my mom wanted to do was hunch over a hot stove. The salad sandwich is just what it sounds like: bread piled with stuff like tomatoes, cucumbers, lettuce, and onion. My mom would add spring onions from her garden and slather the bread with butter and Heinz Salad Cream. The ones I make today aren't much different, though I typically make my own version of salad cream and might occasionally add boiled eggs with oozy yolks or use goat's cheese butter. Sometimes I'll even bake my own white bread. But really, the little details are up to you.

Fill a medium pot at least halfway with water and bring it to a boil over high heat. Use a slotted spoon to gently add the eggs to the water and cook them for 7 minutes (set a timer), then run them under cold water until they're fully cooled. Lightly tap each egg against the counter to crack the shell all over, then carefully peel them. Slice them however you'd like just before you add them to the sandwich.

Lay the tomato, cucumber and onion in more or less one layer on a large platter or cutting board. Squeeze a little lemon juice over the veg, then add a good drizzle of olive oil and a sprinkle of salt. Flip them over and rub them gently, just to make sure they're all seasoned.

Spread each slice of bread with butter. Layer the tomato, cucumber, onion, lettuce, salad cream, and eggs on 4 slices of bread: I like to start with the tomatoes, then lettuce, then a good old slather of salad cream, then the eggs, the cucumber, and finally the onion. Top with the remaining bread and give each sandwich a firm but gentle press with your palm. Eat straightaway.

makes 4

4 large eggs

450g tomatoes, cut into 0.5-cm thick slices

1 medium crunchy cucumber with minimal seeds, thinly sliced

12 or so rings red onion or 24 or so rings red spring onions

½ lemon

A good drizzle extra-virgin olive oil

Maldon or another flaky sea salt

Eight 1-cm thick slices white bread

A few knobs butter, at room temperature

225g Little Gem lettuce (about 2 heads) or another crunchy lettuce, root end and floppy outer leaves discarded, cut into 0.5-cm thick slices

About 3 tablespoons Salad Cream (page 237)

# STEAMED AND RAW RADISH SALAD WITH KIMCHI AND SESAME

I'm no Korean mother in the kitchen, but I can't get enough of Korean food. So I thought I'd have a bit of fun with three of my favourite Korean ingredients – sesame, radish, and kimchi. Because I'm an Englishwoman with an Englishwoman's palate, the salad I came up with is a quiet one, not full of the fermented fireworks you might expect from Mom. Because I love radishes so very much, I chose to showcase their sweet, sharp bite in a mellow, mouth-fillingly flavourful sesame dressing. I like that in some bites, however, you do get a hit of spicy, funky kimchi.

Put a steamer insert (or a colander, so long as the pot's lid can still close) in a large pot with a lid. Add about 1cm water to the pot, pop on the lid, and bring to a boil over high heat. Add the daikon radishes to the insert, cover again, and let them steam until they're fully tender but not mushy, 12 to 15 minutes. Remove the daikon and let it cool. Put the steamed and raw radishes in the fridge to chill for about 15 minutes.

Meanwhile, put the sesame seeds in a small frying pan. Set it over medium heat and toast, stirring and tossing frequently, until they're a few shades darker, 3 to 5 minutes. Transfer them to a bowl to cool. Set 1 teaspoon of the seeds aside and pour the rest into a mortar, along with a pinch of salt. Thoroughly pound the seeds, add 1 tablespoon of the neutral oil and stir until smooth.

Pulse half of the drained kimchi in a small food processor until you have a coarse purée. Transfer it to a bowl and mix in the rest of the kimchi, the kimchi liquid, the sesame oil, the remaining 3 tablespoons of the neutral oil, and 1 teaspoon of salt.

Combine the kimchi mixture, steamed radishes, raw radishes, and Little Gem leaves in a large bowl and toss well. Season to taste with salt and transfer the vegetables to a plate in a heap. Drizzle the sesame paste mixture over the vegetables, then sprinkle on the remaining sesame seeds.

serves 4 to 6 as a side

350g daikon radishes (each no thicker than 4cm), peeled, topped, tailed and cut into 2.5-cm irregularly shaped pieces

450g mixed small radishes (some with pert greens left on), halved lengthwise if larger than 2.5cm in diameter

2 tablespoons plus 1 teaspoon sesame seeds

Maldon or another flaky sea salt

4 tablespoons neutral oil, such as safflower or grapeseed

150g roughly chopped drained kimchi (preferably homemade, page 225), plus 2 tablespoons of the kimchi liquid

1 teaspoon toasted sesame oil

1 head Little Gem lettuce, root end and floppy outer leaves discarded, leaves separated

# ROASTED CAULIFLOWER AND GRAIN SALAD WITH PISTACHIOS AND POMEGRANATE

When I make salads, I try to make sure every bite keeps the diner interested. Here, that means putting together a bunch of elements – aromatic roasted cauliflower, the snappy grains, the sweet-salty onions, rich pistachios, and tart, crunchy pomegranate seeds – to ensure each mouthful is a bit different from the last. The list of ingredients for this recipe might be lengthy, but I promise this salad isn't hard to make and is well worth the effort it requires. You can simmer the grains while the cauliflower is roasting and the onions are getting soft and sweet in a pan. And if you must, you can store the grains, cauliflower, and onions in the fridge overnight and let them come to room temperature before assembling the salad.

Position a rack in the centre of the oven and preheat to 230°C/gas 8.

Combine the raisins and carrot juice in a small bowl and set it aside. Toast the coriander seeds in a small pan over medium-high heat, shaking the pan frequently, until they smell really warm and inviting, 3 to 5 minutes. Grind the seeds to a powder in a spice grinder or pound them in a mortar.

Combine the cauliflower in a large mixing bowl with the garlic, chillies, 55ml of the olive oil, 1 heaped teaspoon of the salt and 2 teaspoons of the ground coriander (reserve the rest for the final step). Toss well to coat the cauliflower in oil and spices and spread the mixture out in a single layer in a large, heavy enamelled baking dish. Add 55ml of water to the bowl, swish it around to get at any stubborn spices, and pour it into the baking dish (around, not over, the cauliflower).

Cover the dish tightly with foil and pop it into the oven. Cook until the cauliflower is tender with a slight bite and the water is all gone, about

serves 6 as a side

100g golden raisins

55ml carrot juice

1 tablespoon coriander seeds

1 medium head cauliflower, trimmed and cut into florets (about 5 x 5cm)

2 medium garlic cloves, very finely chopped

3 dried pequín chillies, crumbled, or pinches of red pepper flakes

55ml plus 5 tablespoons extra-virgin olive oil

Generous 2 teaspoons plus a healthy pinch of Maldon or another flaky sea salt

1 medium red onion (about 225g), halved and thinly sliced

500g cooked grain, such as freekeh, farro, pearl barley, rye berries or brown rice

30g unsalted roasted pistachios, coarsely chopped

30g pomegranate seeds

15 minutes. Remove the foil and continue cooking, stirring now and then, until the cauliflower is browned in spots and fully tender but not mushy, about 8 minutes more. Transfer the cauliflower to a plate and let cool to room temperature.

Heat 2 tablespoons of the oil in a medium cast-iron frying pan over medium-high heat until the oil smokes lightly. Add the onion, stir well, and cook, stirring often and near the end scraping the pan frequently so nothing burns, until the onion is very soft, sweet, and dark brown at the edges, about 15 minutes. Add 1 teaspoon of the salt, stir well, and transfer to a large mixing bowl to cool to room temperature.

Add the roasted cauliflower to the cooled onion. Add the cooked grains, pistachios, pomegranate seeds, preserved lemon, lemon juice, remaining 3 tablespoons of oil, the reserved ground coriander, the soaked raisins (including any remaining carrot juice) and a healthy pinch or two of salt.

Toss the mint and parsley together on the cutting board and very coarsely chop them. Add the herbs to the mixing bowl, toss everything gently but well with your hands, and serve.

1 tablespoon finely chopped preserved lemon rind (from 1 very small preserved lemon, flesh and pith discarded)

2 tablespoons lemon juice

A small handful of mint leaves

A small handful of delicate flat-leaf parsley sprigs

*satisfying salads* **89**

# BEAN AND MUSHROOM SALAD

This is the sort of salad I'd make at home. It's a bit more refined than your average salad – a few components prepared separately and assembled just before you eat – but still uncomplicated and satisfying enough to serve as a meal for two along with a bit of bread. Feel free to use this recipe as a jumping-off point for your own twist on things. Black trumpets and girolles are swell, but so are portobello mushrooms. Canned beans work in a pinch, so long as they're perked up with vinegar and lashed with olive oil. And whatever greens you use, be sure they're good and sturdy, so they can stand up to the warm beans and mushrooms.

2 teaspoons plus 3 tablespoons extra-virgin olive oil, plus several glugs for the greens

300g mixed girolle and black trumpet mushrooms, cleaned (see 'Cleaning Wild Mushrooms', page 135)

2 tablespoons unsalted butter

1 medium garlic clove, finely chopped

A small handful of delicate flat-leaf parsley sprigs, leaves coarsely chopped, stems thinly sliced

Maldon or another flaky sea salt

1 lemon, halved

75g Simple Beans (page 244), plus 225ml of their tasty liquid

2 teaspoons sherry or Banyuls vinegar (available at specialty shops and online)

3 large handfuls of torn sturdy mixed greens and chicories (about 225g), such as stemmed Tuscan kale and radicchio

### cook the mushrooms

Heat about 1 teaspoon of oil (just enough to thinly coat the bottom of the pan) in a large cast-iron frying pan over high heat until it smokes. Add half the mushrooms and cook, stirring frequently, until the mushrooms have wilted and are no longer raw, about 1 minute. Transfer the mushrooms to a bowl, wipe out the pan, add about another teaspoon of oil, and repeat with the remaining mushrooms. Let the frying pan cool.

Wipe out the frying pan again and set it over high heat. Add the butter, let it melt a bit, then add the garlic and cook, stirring, just until it begins to brown, about 20 seconds. Add the parsley, give the pan a good shake, then add the cooked mushrooms. Cook for a minute, stirring often, then add a healthy pinch of salt, and keep cooking until the mushrooms have a kiss of brown, 1 to 2 minutes more. Take the pan off the heat and squeeze on just enough lemon to add brightness but not acidity. Set the pan aside for the moment.

### assemble the salad

Combine the beans and bean liquid, the vinegar, 3 tablespoons of the oil, and ½ teaspoon of salt in a medium frying pan. Set it over high heat and bring the liquid to a strong simmer, shaking and swirling the pan regularly (if you stir, you risk breaking the beans), until the mixture looks glossy but isn't gloppy, about 5 minutes. Take the pan off the heat.

Toss the greens in a large bowl with a few glugs of olive oil, a healthy squeeze of lemon and a sprinkle of salt. Transfer them to a platter or large plate, then spoon on the beans and mushrooms here and there.

*satisfying salads*

# ROASTED AND RAW FENNEL SALAD WITH BLOOD ORANGE AND BOTTARGA

Any time a vegetable is as tasty raw as it is cooked, it's fun to explore combining its different sides in one salad. For example, I'm big on the crunch and perfume of raw fennel. But I also love the way roasting fennel gives it a meaty texture as well as a sweeter, more concentrated, and more complex taste. When you combine the two preparations – along with fennel seeds, pollen, and fronds to add even more layers of flavour – the salad goes from just another nice dish on your table to the meal's main event.

Position a rack in the centre of the oven and preheat to 230°C/gas 8.

Halve two of the fennel bulbs through the root end, then cut them through the root nub (so each wedge stays intact) into approximately 2.5-cm thick wedges. Combine the wedges in a mixing bowl with the garlic, fennel seeds, chillies, 55ml of the oil, ½ teaspoon of the salt and 55ml of water, and toss well. Spread the mixture in a heavy enamelled baking dish (large enough to hold the fennel in a single layer with a little room to spare) and cover tightly with foil. Roast the fennel until it is tender (it should meet with almost no resistance when poked with a knife) and golden brown on the bottom, 25 to 30 minutes. Remove the foil and roast just until the golden brown colour gets a shade or so darker, 3 to 5 minutes more. Let the fennel cool to room temperature.

Meanwhile, halve one of the oranges and squeeze 3 tablespoons of juice into a small bowl. Use a sharp knife to cut off just enough of the top and bottom of the remaining oranges to expose a full circle of the flesh on either side. Stand them on a flat end, and cut along the border where the flesh meets the pith, following the curve of the fruit to remove the pith and peel. Repeat the process until all you have left are nice round, naked fruits. If you've missed any white pith, trim it off. Slice the fruit crosswise into 0.5-cm thick rounds. Flick out any seeds.

serves 4 to 6 as a side

4 large fennel bulbs, stalks and outermost layer discarded, tender fronds reserved, root end trimmed of brown bits

2 medium garlic cloves, finely chopped

½ teaspoon fennel seeds, coarsely crushed in a mortar

3 dried pequín chillies, crumbled, or pinches of red pepper flakes

55ml plus 2 tablespoons extra-virgin olive oil

1½ teaspoons Maldon or another flaky sea salt

4 blood oranges

1 tablespoon lemon juice

Several turns of freshly ground black pepper

A handful of delicate, peppery rocket

50g unsalted roasted pistachios, very coarsely crushed

1 teaspoon fennel pollen

1 ounce *bottarga di muggine* (salted mullet roe), finely grated

To the blood orange juice in the bowl, whisk in the lemon juice, the pepper, the remaining 2 tablespoons of oil, and 1 teaspoon of salt.

Slice the remaining 2 fennel bulbs crosswise into 0.5-cm thick slices (only remove the core if it's very tough) and separate the layers with your fingers. Toss the raw fennel, roasted fennel (and any oil and browned bits left in the pan), and dressing in a large mixing bowl. Use your hands to give it all a gentle scrunch – just to help the flavours come together.

Very coarsely chop enough of the reserved fennel fronds to give you a handful. Add the fronds, rocket and pistachios to the bowl and toss again.

Spoon some of the fennel mixture onto a platter, arrange some blood orange slices here and there, then add another layer of fennel and oranges. Sprinkle on the fennel pollen, bottarga and, if you'd like, a healthy pinch of salt. Serve straightaway.

*simple things*

# fennel

I suppose boiled fennel doesn't sound all that appetising. It's true, raw fennel has a fantastic crunch, entrancing perfume, and delicate, feminine sweetness. But after it's had a nice bath in salty boiling water, it goes subtle, creamy, and a bit juicy. And that's my favourite way to eat the veg.

Next time you come across some – I like the especially bulbous variety called Florence fennel, and don't care for baby fennel – grab a few bulbs and get to work. Bring plenty of water to a boil and add to it a good handful of sea salt. The water should taste quite salty, though not as salty as the sea. The bigger your bulbs, the more heavily you should salt your water. Remove the stalks and tough outer layer of the fennel and consider saving them for stock. Trim any brown bits from the root end, but keep the root intact. Halve the bulbs through the root and plunk them in the water. They're ready when you can cut them with a spoon.

While the fennel cooks, take some of the feathery fronds – from the centre of the cluster, where they're especially sweet – and coarsely chop them. Drain the fennel, pat it dry, arrange it on a plate, and season with flaky sea salt, a little crumbled dried chilli, a light drizzle of good olive oil and a few drops of lemon juice – just to add a bit of brightness. Finish the dish by sprinkling on the fronds – they add back a little of that fresh sweet flavour the boiling stole.

summer, lovely summer

# IF-IT-AIN'T-BROKE AUBERGINE CAPONATA

I learned to make caponata at the River Café in London, and as with many things I learned to make there, their version became the one to which I aspire whenever I make caponata today. Before the River Café, I had a problem with caponata. I'm not big on the raisins that wind up in so many renditions. I don't like the common addition of sugar, either – the artificial sweetness makes me shudder. But Rose and Ruth turned to ripe tomatoes and slowly cooked onion and celery for natural and more complex sweetness. Rather than a ton of vinegar, they found brightness in just a touch of it along with celery leaves and olives. And they taught me one of those kitchen tricks that can change how you see an ingredient – before cooking the aubergine, I learned to salt it and then drain off some of its liquid. The magical result? It doesn't absorb nearly as much oil when it cooks. The pieces of aubergine turn out creamy, rather than greasy and mushy. All in all, I barely tinker with their recipe. Why fix what isn't broken?

Toss the aubergine and sea salt together in a colander and set the colander over a bowl. Let the aubergine sit for about 30 minutes.

Meanwhile, quarter the tomatoes and trim off any pale bits. Hold each chunk over a bowl, and use your fingers to push out the juice and seeds. Strain the juice, discarding the seeds. Finely chop the tomatoes.

Heat 3 tablespoons of the oil in a medium pot over medium-high heat until it shimmers. Add the onion, celery, garlic, and 1 teaspoon of the Maldon salt. Cook, stirring and scraping occasionally, until the onion is translucent and begins to stick to the pot, about 10 minutes. Lower the heat to medium and cook the vegetables for another 10 minutes. Add the chillies and keep cooking, stirring and scraping occasionally, until the vegetables are light brown, soft and sweet, about 10 minutes more. Stir in the tomatoes and their strained juice and let the mixture simmer, stirring now and then, for about 15 minutes.

serves 6 to 8 as a side

900g large aubergines, unpeeled, topped, tailed and cut into about 4-cm pieces

½ tablespoon sea salt

450g tomatoes, peeled (see page 16) and cored

110ml plus 3 tablespoons extra-virgin olive oil

1 medium Spanish onion (about 225g), finely chopped

560g celery, bottoms trimmed, stalks cut into 1-cm irregularly shaped pieces, inner leaves reserved and roughly chopped

3 medium garlic cloves, thinly sliced

Maldon or another flaky sea salt

4 dried pequín chillies, crumbled, or pinches of red pepper flakes

1 tablespoon red wine vinegar

45g Niçoise olives (or a mixture of varieties), smashed with the flat of a knife, pits removed and very roughly chopped

Pat the aubergine dry. Heat the remaining 110ml of olive oil in a medium cast-iron frying pan over medium heat until it shimmers. Cook the aubergine in two batches to avoid crowding the pan, turning the pieces often and adjusting the heat if necessary, until they're deep golden brown on the outside and creamy inside, 10 to 12 minutes per batch. Put the aubergine on paper towels to drain. Let it cool to warm.

Transfer the aubergine to a large bowl, sprinkle with the vinegar and a pinch or two of Maldon salt, and give a very light stir, being careful not to smoosh the pieces. To the bowl, add the tomato mixture, olives, pine nuts, capers, basil, and a small handful of the reserved celery leaves. Have another gentle stir, and season to taste with Maldon salt.

The caponata will keep in an airtight container in the fridge for up to 3 days, but you should always serve it at room temperature.

35g pine nuts, lightly toasted

2 tablespoons drained capers, roughly chopped

A five-finger pinch of basil leaves, roughly chopped at the last minute

# EGGS IN PIPÉRADE

Pipérade is Basque cooking at its simplest. Little more than tomatoes, onions and peppers cooked together in olive oil, the dish relies on good ingredients and a careful cook. Peeling the peppers allows them to develop a meaty texture. Scraping off the sweet bits of onions and pepper that cling to the pot means they'll never go too dark and turn bitter. The addition of eggs turns it from sauce to a one-pot meal. You may prefer to scramble the eggs with the pipérade or perhaps make an omelette and spoon some of it on top. I like to crack the eggs straight into the pot and let them cook just until the whites have set and the yolks are still good and runny. Whatever way you choose, don't eat this without plenty of toast for mopping up that sauce.

Peel the skin from the peppers using a vegetable peeler and a gentle sawing motion. Slice the peppers into long strips that are somewhere between 0.5 and 1cm thick. Set them aside.

Heat the 55ml of oil in a large casserole or heavy cast-iron frying pan over medium heat until it shimmers. Add the onion and 1 teaspoon of the salt. Cook, stirring occasionally, until the onion has softened, about 5 minutes. Push the onion to one side of the pot and add the garlic to the oil. Cook, stirring the garlic occasionally but not the onions, until the garlic turns light golden and smells toasty, about 3 minutes. Stir it all together and cook, stirring now and then, until the onion is lightly browned and very soft, 6 to 8 minutes.

Add the peppers to the pot along with the remaining 1 teaspoon of the salt and cook, stirring often and scraping the bottom after a while, until the onions start to disintegrate and the peppers are tender but not at all mushy, about 10 minutes.

Reduce the heat to medium-low and keep cooking, stirring and scraping, until the pot gets lovely brown sticky stuff on it and the peppers get a bit softer, about 5 minutes more. Have a taste. The

**serves 2 as a main**

900g mixed yellow and red peppers (about 4 medium), halved lengthwise, seeded and deribbed

55ml extra-virgin olive oil, plus a healthy drizzle for finishing

1 medium red onion (about 225g), halved and thinly sliced

2 teaspoons Maldon or another flaky sea salt

2 medium garlic cloves, thinly sliced

225g Simple Tomato Sauce (page 242), at room temperature

A five-finger pinch of basil leaves, roughly chopped, plus more for finishing

3 large eggs

5 dried pequín chillies, crumbled, or pinches of red pepper flakes

peppers should be really sweet and have a meaty texture. Stir in the tomato sauce and cook at a good sizzle until it thickens slightly, a few minutes. Stir in 110ml of water and the basil and let the mixture return to a simmer. Season to taste with salt.

Add the eggs to the pot, cover with a lid, and reduce the heat to low. Cook until the eggs are to your liking, 4 to 5 minutes for nice runny yolks. Sprinkle the chillies on the yolks, scatter on the rest of the basil, drizzle on some olive oil and serve straightaway.

# PIEDMONTESE PEPPERS WITH TOMATO, BASIL AND ANCHOVY

The clever cooking method is just one reason to love so-called Piedmontese peppers. Halved peppers act as little tubs that hold a whole tomato, an anchovy fillet, a basil leaf and a few slivers of garlic. As the peppers roast, the tomatoes nesting inside them release a bit of juice, transforming the peppers into hot tubs. The main reason, though, is the result: next thing you know, the flesh of the peppers is creamy and their edges are toasty. The tomatoes' flavour becomes concentrated, and their anchovy-infused juice is sweet, aromatic, and full of umami. I'd happily eat these as is, but you could serve them with some mozzarella or burrata on the side, bread spread with pesto, or alongside lightly dressed rocket.

You want to find tomatoes that are small enough to fit inside the pepper halves but large enough that they rise above the sides. Of course, you can cut larger tomatoes to fit, adding them rounded side up, though the dish will look a little less sexy.

Position a rack in the centre of the oven and preheat to 230°C/gas 8.

Find a heavy enamelled baking dish that will fit the peppers snugly and arrange them cut sides up. To each half, add 2 or 3 slices of garlic, an anchovy fillet, a basil leaf, and finally a tomato.

Sprinkle on the salt, add several grindings of pepper, and evenly drizzle the olive oil over everything. Pop the dish in the oven and cook until the edges of the peppers go wrinkly and a bit toasty and the flesh is creamy, 45 minutes to 1 hour. After 20 minutes and every 10 minutes or so thereafter, give the tomatoes a gentle press with the back of a spoon so a little juice squeezes out, then baste the peppers.

Remove the peppers from the oven and let them rest in the baking dish until they're just a bit warmer than room temperature. Baste them once more, then carefully transfer the peppers to plates or a platter, drizzle on the liquid remaining in the pan, and sprinkle on the torn basil.

serves 6 to 8 as a side

8 small red peppers (about 1.3kg), halved lengthwise, seeded and deribbed, green stem nubs left intact

3 medium garlic cloves, thinly sliced

8 salt-packed whole anchovies, soaked and filleted (see page 13)

16 large basil leaves, plus extra, torn, for finishing

16 small to medium tomatoes (about 900g), peeled (see page 16) and cored

1 tablespoon Maldon or another flaky sea salt

Freshly ground black pepper

A healthy drizzle of extra-virgin olive oil

# simple things
# tomatoes

I love a good tomato table, the spread a proud farmer sets out at her market stand. I love reading the eccentric names of the varieties scribbled on scraps of paper: Striped German, Green Zebra, Brandywine, Cherokee Purple. Some people have a favourite variety, but I like them all. So how do I decide what to buy on any given day? I start by inspecting all the tomatoes and choosing whichever ones are heavy and firm with a slight give. From those I pick the most vividly coloured tomatoes, and from those I choose ones where the colour (or mottling, in the case of certain heirloom varieties) is the same everywhere, even near the eye, where lesser tomatoes are often pale.

Once at home, I don't do much at all to them. A sprinkle of flaky sea salt. Perhaps a drizzle of olive oil and a few shreds of torn basil. A squeeze of lemon if the tomatoes are quite sweet. My mood determines the way I slice them. If I'm relaxed, I choose thin slices, which give the tomatoes a silky texture as they sort of glide over your tongue. If I'm eager to shove them in my gob, I chop them into good old chunks. They're nice and meaty that way. Either way, a sharp knife is essential: a dull knife will make ragged cuts or even worse, mush the tomatoes.

# SUMMERY RIBOLLITA

This classic Tuscan soup is the result of clever cooks who stretched leftover minestrone by adding stale bread. They brought the whole mess to a boil (*ribollita* means 're-boiled' in Italian) and the bread melted, thickening the broth and turning something unassuming into something special. Nowadays, cooks like me have come to love ribollita so much they make it from scratch. Like most simple dishes, it takes a bit of care to get right. The steps are not meant to torment you, I promise. Each has a purpose that you'll taste in the final product. The vegetables must be chopped nice and small, so they'll almost disappear into the soup, and they must be cooked slowly and lovingly to guarantee the soup's complex flavour. You must use beans you've cooked yourself, because their flavourful cooking liquid takes the place of stock. Sweet summer tomatoes must be passed through a food mill to add silkiness. (Well, 'must' is a strong word.) At the end of summer, you might decide to swap chard for another delicate, herbaceous leaf like borage, which gardeners often plant between tomatoes to ward off pests. As the weather turns cold, and you crave an even heartier soup, you might add kale instead of chard and top-notch canned tomatoes instead of fresh. You might also take the onions, carrots and celery past light brown into deeper, darker territory.

Combine the whole garlic cloves and marjoram on a cutting board and finely chop together until the mixture looks a bit like blue cheese.

Heat 110ml of the oil in a large pot over medium-high heat until it shimmers. Add the onion, celery, carrot, chard stems, and 1 teaspoon of the salt. Cook, stirring often, for 15 minutes, then stir in the marjoram mixture and the chillies. Reduce the heat to medium-low and cook, stirring often near the end, until the vegetables are very soft, lightly browned and sweet, about 45 minutes.

Meanwhile, pour just enough water into a medium pot to barely cover the bottom. Bring it to a boil, add the chard leaves and pop on a lid. Cook, stirring once, until the leaves are fully wilted and

*serves 4 as a main*

6 medium garlic cloves, peeled, 4 whole, 2 thinly sliced

A small handful of marjoram leaves

110ml plus 3 tablespoons extra-virgin olive oil, plus a few glugs for finishing

1 medium-large Spanish onion (about 350g), finely diced

4 large celery stalks, finely diced

1 large carrot, peeled and finely diced

450g Swiss chard (about 1 bunch), leaves separated from the stalks, stalks finely diced, leaves torn into large pieces

2 teaspoons Maldon salt or another flaky sea salt

3 dried pequín chillies, crumbled, or pinches of red pepper flakes, plus more for finishing

900g cherry tomatoes, each pricked with the tip of a sharp knife tender, about 3 minutes. Drain the chard well and give it a rough chop. Wipe out the pot.

Combine the remaining 3 tablespoons of oil and the thinly sliced garlic in the pot. Set the pot over high heat and cook, stirring, until the garlic turns light golden brown, about 1 minute. Add the tomatoes and remaining 1 teaspoon of salt, then cover the pot and lower the heat to medium. Cook, stirring once or twice, until the tomatoes soften and the skins begin to burst, about 8 minutes. Uncover and mash the tomatoes for a couple of minutes.

Pass the tomato mixture through a food mill into a bowl (or if you must, pass it through a mesh strainer set over the bowl, smooshing and stirring to get as much liquid as you can). Discard the solids. You should have about 450ml of tomato liquid.

Stir the tomato liquid into the pot with the onions, bring it to a simmer over medium heat, and cook for 5 minutes. Add just the beans (reserving the liquid) and continue simmering, stirring occasionally, for a few minutes, just so the ingredients all get to know one another. Stir in the bean liquid, let it come to a simmer, then add the bread to the liquid in one layer. Cook for another 5 minutes or so until the bread begins to melt. Add the chard leaves and stir roughly to help the bread fully melt and thicken the soup. Cook just until the soup is warmed through. If you'd like, add more crumbled chillies, salt, and a few good glugs of olive oil. Serve straightaway.

225g Simple Beans (page 244), including 565ml of their tasty liquid

Scant 225g slightly stale rustic bread, such as filone, crust discarded, pulled into about 2.5-cm pieces

# STEWED COURGETTES WITH BASIL

serves 4 as a side

This dish was inspired by a trip to Rome. After a few days, I was tired of cappuccino and, like a proper Englishwoman, desperate for a cup of tea. (A bit lame, I know.) I popped into a tea shop near the Spanish Steps and ordered a pot. Along with the tea I was served a complimentary snack that turned out to be just about the best thing in the world. The waitress had brought over an English muffin topped with mozzarella and stewed courgette. It was the simplest thing, this courgette: soft chunks coated by a little of the creamy smashed vegetable. It was even made with my favourite variety, Romanesco courgette, which has ridges, speckles, and an earthy quality – a tiny bit like manure, if you ask me.

My version of the dish requires little more than nice courgettes, the kind that are the size of pickling cucumbers, not the fat watery, seedy ones or pinky-size baby ones. Cutting the courgettes into pieces with especially sharp edges means most stay whole, but some break down and coat the others. When summer winds down, I like a little colour on the courgette to give it a warmness and meatiness, as in this recipe. But when the weather's still hot, I prefer none, so I add the salt with the courgette, to draw out its water sooner. It's really up to you, though.

675g small courgettes, topped, tailed and halved lengthwise

55ml extra-virgin olive oil

5 medium garlic cloves, halved lengthwise

1½ teaspoons Maldon or another flaky sea salt

A five-finger pinch of basil leaves, roughly chopped

1 teaspoon lemon juice

½ teaspoon finely grated lemon zest

A few dried pequin chillies, crumbled, or pinches of red pepper flakes (optional)

Cut the courgettes like so: start by cutting a piece on the diagonal that's about 2.5cm long. Turn the courgette about 45 degrees towards you and cut another piece at the same angle. Return the courgette to its original position, cut at the same angle, and so on.

Heat the oil in a medium pot (one with high sides that's wide enough to hold the courgette snugly in about two layers) over high heat until it lightly smokes. Add the courgette, carve out a little space in the pot, and add the garlic. Don't stir just yet. Cook until the garlic is golden and the courgette pieces on the bottom are golden brown, 3 to 5 minutes. (If the garlic is done early, pop it on top of the courgette.)

Have a good stir.

Sprinkle on ½ teaspoon of the salt, reduce the heat to medium-low, and pop on the lid. Cook, stirring occasionally, for 5 minutes or so. Now, take a listen: if you hear the courgette frying in oil rather than simmering in a little liquid, then add 2 tablespoons of water. Pop on the lid again and cook, stirring occasionally, until some of the courgette pieces are tender but not mushy and some are nearly tender, 3 to 5 minutes more.

Stir in the remaining 1 teaspoon of salt and the basil. Cook, without the lid, and every 30 seconds or so use a sturdy whisk or wooden spoon to very roughly stir and strike the courgette, not to smash the pieces but just to knock off some of the points that have gotten soft. Keep at it until some of the softer pieces have broken down and turned creamy and the other pieces are tender with a slight bite, about 3 minutes. Stir in the lemon juice, zest, Chillies, and more salt if you fancy. Eat straight-away.

# COURGETTE BREAD

Carrot cake and pumpkin pie make a strong case for crafting dessert out of vegetables. Unlike carrots and pumpkins, which are quite sugary, courgette is only subtly sweet. This makes me wonder who first thought to turn it into a bread that you eat for pudding. Well, whoever did is a clever one indeed. Somehow the courgette keeps the bread moist and, just as carrots do in cake, provides just a smidgen of its earthy character. My courgette bread includes the brightness of lemon zest, chunks of walnuts, and a little crunchy topping of sugar. A slice (or two) is just the thing with a cup of milky English breakfast tea hot enough to just barely scald the back of your throat.

Position a rack in the centre of the oven and preheat to 180°C/gas 4.

Coat two 23 x 12cm loaf tins with cooking spray. Cut 2 strips of baking parchment that are the width of the bottom of the loaf tin and twice as long. Lay a baking parchment strip in each loaf tin so it completely covers the bottom and hangs over the tin's two short sides.

Spread the walnuts in a single layer on a baking sheet and bake, stirring occasionally, until they're aromatic but not coloured, 6 to 8 minutes. Keep the oven on. Transfer the walnuts to a cutting board to cool, then roughly chop them so you have a mixture of small and large chunks.

Combine the flour, bicarbonate of soda, baking powder and cinnamon in a large bowl and stir well. Give both courgettes a light squeeze with your hands to remove excess surface moisture, lay them on a towel and give them a light pat.

Put the eggs in the bowl of the stand mixer fitted with the paddle attachment and mix on medium speed, gradually adding the granulated sugar and occasionally scraping the sides of the bowl, until the mixture doubles in volume, turns pale and looks like a ribbon as it falls when you lift the paddle, about 5 minutes.

Next, with the mixer running on low speed, add the oil in a slow,

## makes two 23-cm loaves

SPECIAL EQUIPMENT
Two 23 x 12cm loaf tins, a stand mixer with paddle attachment, and a wire rack

90g walnuts

230g plain flour

1½ teaspoons bicarbonate of soda

¼ teaspoon baking powder

2 teaspoons ground cinnamon

290g coarsely grated green courgette (grated on the largest holes of a box grater)

290g coarsely grated yellow courgette (grated on the largest holes of a box grater)

3 large eggs

450g granulated sugar

110ml sunflower or vegetable oil

2 teaspoons vanilla extract

Finely grated zest of 1 large lemon

A five-finger pinch of summer savoury leaves (optional)

Large pinch of Maldon or another flaky sea salt

1 tablespoon demerara sugar

steady stream, then add the courgette, vanilla extract and lemon zest and mix until everything is well combined. Turn off the mixer. Add half the flour mixture to the mixer and mix on low speed until almost incorporated. Turn off the mixer, add the remaining flour mixture and walnuts, then mix again on low speed just until incorporated. Mix too much and the bread will be too dense.

Divide the batter evenly between the two loaf tins. Sprinkle the salt and demerara sugar evenly over the surface of the batter. Bake the loaves until a toothpick inserted into the centre comes out clean, 50 minutes to 1 hour.

Transfer the tins to a wire rack to cool slightly, about 30 minutes, then use the baking parchment overhang to remove the loaves from the tin, running a knife along the edges of the bread if need be. Put the loaves on a wire rack to cool fully.

Wrapped in clingfilm, the bread keeps at room temperature for up to 3 days and in the fridge for up to 1 week.

# CORN SOUP WITH CREAM AND GIROLLE MUSHROOMS

The key to corn soup is finding the sweetest ears you can and then making sure you use every bit of flavour they contain. That means not just slicing the kernels away from the cobs, but also – and this is a really joyful activity – scraping the back of your knife blade down the naked cobs, almost like you're scaling a fish. This gives you a pile of sweet, starchy scrapings that'll add body and flavour to your soup. Then steeping the cobs in the milk and cream means even the dairy gets infused with the corn's essence. For a touch of elegance and to balance all that sweet corn flavour, I top each bowl with sautéed girolle mushrooms.

## make the soup

Cut the corn kernels from the cobs and measure out 1kg of kernels. Use the back of the knife blade to scrape each cob of any bits of kernel left behind. Combine the kernels and scrapings in a bowl, reserving the cobs.

Cut the cobs crosswise into a few pieces and pop them into a medium pot along with the milk and cream. Cover the pot, bring to a boil over high heat, then remove the pot from the heat and let it sit, covered, for at least 5 minutes. Remove the cobs, gently scraping them with a spoon to get at any liquid that may be hiding in them, and discard the cobs.

Melt the butter in a large pot over low heat. When the butter froths, add the shallots and salt, stir, and cover the pot. Cook, stirring now and then, until the shallots are soft and creamy but not coloured, 10 to 12 minutes. Add the corn kernels and scrapings to the pot and stir. Increase the heat to medium, cover the pot, and cook, stirring occasionally, until the kernels are tender but still have a pop, about 10 minutes.

Add the milk mixture to the pot and give everything a stir. Cover and simmer gently over medium-low heat for another 15 minutes to fully

serves 6 to 8

FOR THE SOUP

8 medium ears corn, shucked

675ml whole milk

240ml double cream

6 tablespoons unsalted butter

2 large shallots (about 100g), thinly sliced

1 tablespoon Maldon or another flaky sea salt

FOR THE GARNISH

50g unsalted butter

175g fresh girolle mushrooms, cleaned (see 'Cleaning Wild Mushrooms', page 135) and halved through the stem if wider than a penny

½ teaspoon Maldon or another flaky sea salt

½ lemon

2 tablespoons thinly sliced chives

A healthy drizzle of extra-virgin olive oil

soften the kernels and infuse the liquid with corn flavour. Pour the soup into a large mixing bowl. Working in batches, blend the mixture (be careful when blending hot liquids) until very smooth, adding each batch back to the pot. Keep the soup warm over very low heat for the moment.

### prepare the garnish

Melt the butter in a medium cast-iron frying pan over medium-low heat. When the butter froths, add the mushrooms and salt, have a stir, then cover the frying pan. Cook the mushrooms, stirring occasionally, just until they're tender and their liquid has melded with the butter to make a simple pan sauce, about 5 minutes. Gently squeeze on just enough lemon juice so that when you taste a girolle, you taste its earthy flavour first and a pop of acidity second.

Ladle the soup into bowls. Top each with a spoonful of mushrooms, a drizzle of the pan sauce, a sprinkle of chives and a drizzle of olive oil. Serve straightaway.

# CORN PUDDING

I figure that calling this dish corn pudding, even though some might call it soufflé, will encourage any home cooks put off by soufflé's reputation for being difficult. The recipe certainly isn't. So long as you use the sweetest corn you can find and make sure you're gentle with your fluffy egg whites, then you'll have a pudding that puffs up in golden brown patches so stunningly that your mates might mention that the pudding reminds them of a soufflé. Just smile and nod.

Position a rack in the centre of the oven and preheat to 200°C/gas 6.

Cut the corn kernels from the cobs. Use the back of the knife blade to scrape each cob of any bits of kernel left behind. Transfer the kernels and scrapings to a small pot. Discard the cobs.

Add the cream and milk to the pot and bring the liquid to a boil over medium-high heat. Lower the heat to maintain a gentle simmer and cook until the kernels are tender with a slight bite, about 3 minutes. Stir in the salt. Transfer about half the mixture to a blender and purée until very smooth. Add the remaining corn mixture to the blender and stir well.

Clean the pot and set it over medium-low heat. Add the butter and let it melt and froth a little, then add the flour, whisking until the mixture is fully smooth. Cook, stirring constantly, for a minute or so, so the flour loses its raw flavour. Increase the heat to medium, gradually add the corn mixture, a ladleful at a time, stirring constantly and letting the mixture come to a simmer before adding the next ladleful. Let the mixture cool fully. (If you'd like, speed up the cooling by transferring the mixture to a medium bowl, nesting that bowl in a larger one half filled with very icy water, and stirring frequently.) Thoroughly whisk in the egg yolks.

Generously butter the inside of a 1.5-litre, 5-cm deep round or oval baking dish. Beat the egg whites to stiff peaks in a stainless steel bowl, then carefully use a stainless steel spoon to tenderly fold the whites

serves 4 to 6 as a side

SPECIAL EQUIPMENT
A 1.5-litre, 5-cm deep round or oval baking dish

3 large ears corn, shucked

240ml double cream

110ml whole milk

1½ tablespoons Maldon or another flaky sea salt

3 tablespoons unsalted butter, at room temperature, cut into several pieces, plus more for the baking dish

2 tablespoons plain flour

4 large eggs, yolks and whites separated

into the corn mixture. You don't want to lose too much of the air you beat into the whites by stirring too much or too roughly. It's fine if you still see streaks of egg whites. Gently scrape it all into the baking dish.

Put the baking dish in a larger baking dish or roasting pan and put it on the oven rack. Carefully pour enough hot water into the larger dish to reach three-quarters of the way up the sides of the smaller dish. Bake, covering loosely with foil after 30 minutes or so if the top is threatening to get dark brown, until the pudding puffs up in golden and golden-brown patches and is just set but still jiggly in the centre, 45 to 55 minutes. Let it cool in the water bath just until you can remove the dish with your hands. Serve while it's still warm.

*vegetable pastas, polenta,
pastries and friends*

# FRESH EGG PASTA

When you've made your own pasta, you don't have to do much else to arrive somewhere delicious. Just some butter, black pepper and a touch of cream would make me happy. Yet fresh pasta is also a fantastic way to make use of the season's bounty. In the spring, when asparagus has at last arrived, I add juicy boiled slivers to noodles and sauce it all with luxurious *fonduta* (see page 133). When autumn comes and with it girolles, I look to pasta to transform them (see page 134) into dinner.

If you haven't yet had a go at making pasta yourself, you're in for a treat. Not only will you be surprised that you can produce such delicate noodles at home, but if you're anything like me you'll also find yourself enjoying the process – the gratifying exertion of kneading the dough until it's as smooth as a baby's bum, the satisfaction of watching the blob of dough become thin sheets as you feed it through a pasta roller. Speaking of rollers, I don't love using electric ones to roll out pasta. Once you start feeding the machine, the rolling happens quite quickly, which puts you under a lot of pressure. I prefer a hand-crank device, which lets you go at your own pace.

Everyone has her own preferences for pasta. I like mine quite eggy, with lots of yolks providing richness and a beautiful yellow colour. And I like a mixture of especially fine '00' flour and semolina, which strikes the right balance of texture between silkiness and chewiness.

## make the dough

Combine the flours and salt in a large bowl and stir well. Pour the mixture onto a clean work surface, make it into a mound, and use a spoon or your fingers to carve out a big well in the centre that's big enough to hold the whole egg and egg yolks. Add the egg and yolks to the well.

Use a fork, holding the tines parallel to your work surface, to break the yolks and stir the eggs in a circular motion. As you stir, you'll see flour from the walls of your well tumbling into the egg. Keep stirring, gradually incorporating the flour into the eggs and occasionally

**makes about 550g**

SPECIAL EQUIPMENT

A hand-cranked pasta machine or a stand mixer with a pasta-roller attachment

185g fine semolina flour, plus more for dusting

185g '00' or 'doppio zero' flour, plus more for dusting

⅛ teaspoon sea salt

1 large egg

12 large egg yolks

gathering the border of flour closer to the slowly expanding bright yellow centre. After 4 minutes or so, you should have a very wet dough surrounded by flour. Now use your hands or a dough scraper to slowly incorporate the rest of the flour, folding and pressing until it's all incorporated.

Cut the dough in half. Knead one piece at a time, keeping the other wrapped in clingfilm, by pressing firmly down and forward with your palm (one hand on top of the other for force), then folding the dough back onto itself, pushing down and forward again, and turning the dough and doing it all over. Keep at it until the dough is smooth like a baby's bum, 5 to 7 minutes. Kneading will prove more challenging as you work the gluten, so you might occasionally switch to the other piece of dough, wrapping the one you're not kneading in clingfilm and letting it relax a bit. Wrap each half in clingfilm and let them rest for at least 20 minutes or up to 1 hour.

### roll out the pasta
Cut each piece of dough in half, rolling out one and keeping the other pieces you aren't working with wrapped in clingfilm. (As you get more comfortable with the process, you might not need to halve them.)

Work with one piece of dough at a time. Form the dough into a rough rectangle that's about 10 x 15cm. Set the rollers to the widest setting and feed the dough through twice. (If the dough feels at all sticky or doesn't come cleanly from the machine, dust it with a little flour.) Set the rollers to their second-widest setting and feed the dough through once. Continue in this manner until the dough has been through each setting once. This process works the gluten in the dough, giving the pasta a lovely texture. At this point, it's fine if the long sheet of dough looks ragged or uneven.

Fold the sheet of pasta onto itself several times to form a rough rectangle (about 12 x 20cm) and press firmly with your hands so the layers stick together. Set the rollers to the widest setting again. Feed the dough through once at each setting until you reach about halfway to the narrowest one. Then start feeding the dough through twice at each setting, continuing toward the narrowest one, until your dough is about 15 x 90cm and about 1 millimetre thick. Cover the dough with a damp towel and repeat with the remaining dough.

for tagliatelle Cut the long sheets crosswise into smaller, shorter sections that are as long as you'd like your pasta to be. I like my tagliatelle to be 30 to 40cm long. Dust each side with semolina, giving the dough a light rub, and stack the sheets neatly. Cut the stack lengthwise into 1-cm wide slices. Gently toss the slices, separating them into individual noodles as you do.

for pappardelle Follow the instructions for tagliatelle, but cut the stack into 2.5-cm wide slices.

for cannelloni Cut the sheets into roughly 10 x 15cm rectangles. There's no need to make them perfect.

At this point the pasta is ready to cook, but I like to leave it on the counter or a tray for 30 minutes or so to dry out a bit. (The drier the pasta, the more time it'll take to cook and the more time you'll have to do any last-minute prep.) You can store it in a plastic storage container (in a loose tangle for tagliatelle and pappardelle, in a stack with a piece of baking parchment between each layer for cannelloni) in the refrigerator for up to 2 days.

# TAGLIATELLE WITH ASPARAGUS AND PARMESAN FONDUTA

This entire dish is right out of Rose and Ruthie's River Café playbook, with just a few tweaks of my own. They taught me how to make fonduta, a silky sauce rich with crème fraîche and egg yolks. It takes less time and just a bit more effort than tomato sauce, and turns a plate of pasta into an elegant and impressive meal. Get yourself some asparagus spears that are as thick as your index finger – not those thin or sprouty ones – and you'll enjoy the juicy slivers in each bite.

Bring a large pot of water to a boil.

Meanwhile, bring a couple of centimetres of water to the boil in a small pot. Whisk together the egg yolks, crème fraîche, Parmesan, and garlic in a large heatproof bowl that will fit snugly in the pot without making contact with the boiling water.

Set the bowl in the small pot and whisk the egg mixture constantly, occasionally scraping the sides and removing the bowl from the pot every couple of minutes as you whisk to keep the cooking nice and slow (don't let it bubble). The mixture will look thick and clumpy for a few seconds, then become liquidy, and then, once the cheese has melted, silky smooth. Cook just until the liquidy sauce has thickened slightly (it should thinly coat the back of a spoon), 6 to 8 minutes. Set the bowl aside in a warm place.

Salt the large pot of boiling water generously until it tastes slightly less salty than the sea. If you're confident that the pasta and asparagus will finish cooking at the same time, add them both to the water. If you're a worrywart, cook the asparagus first, scoop it into a colander to drain, then cook the pasta. Cook the asparagus until it is juicy with a slight bite, 3 to 4 minutes; and cook the pasta until it is fully cooked, 3 to 4 minutes.

Drain the pasta and asparagus well in a colander, then pop them back into the now-empty pot. Pour in most of the fonduta and toss gently but well. Season to taste with salt and more fonduta, if you'd like. Transfer to bowls, top with a little more Parmesan, and eat straightaway.

serves 4 as a main

2 large egg yolks

350g crème fraîche

150g Parmesan cheese, finely grated, plus a bit more for finishing

1 medium garlic clove, finely grated

Sea salt

450g asparagus, woody bottoms snapped off, stalks cut on the diagonal into long 1-cm thick pieces, tips left whole

½ recipe Fresh Egg Pasta (page 127), cut into tagliatelle

# PAPPARDELLE WITH GIROLLE MUSHROOMS

Like ramps and truffles, girolles resist cultivation. They're one of the few remaining foods that only grow wild. And so they're available for a short time and you must pay dearly for them. Dearly but gladly, if you ask me. Of the two main varieties, golden and yellow foot, I much prefer the denser golden girolles that pop up in markets in late summer to early autumn to the skinny, rather watery yellow foots that come around in winter. When cooking golden girolles, there's no better strategy than keeping things simple. At all costs, you want to avoid masking their earthy, fruity (reminiscent of apricots!) flavour by meddling too much. So I apply one of my favourite trios of ingredients – garlic, butter, parsley – and serve the girolles with eggy homemade pasta, all of which keep the spotlight on those wild, wonderful mushrooms.

Bring a large pot of water to a boil and salt the water generously until it tastes slightly less salty than the sea. Leave small girolles (those with caps smaller than a penny) whole. Cut the others lengthwise into 0.5-cm thick slices so that you get some that show off the mushroom's pretty silhouette.

Heat the oil in a large, heavy cast-iron frying pan over medium-high heat until it smokes lightly. Add the garlic and cook, stirring frequently, until the garlic is golden brown and smells toasty, 30 seconds to 1 minute. Reduce the heat to medium-low, add the butter, and let it melt and froth. Add the mushrooms and 1 teaspoon of Maldon salt, have a stir, then cover the frying pan. Cook, stirring occasionally, just until the mushrooms are tender, 2 to 3 minutes. Add 125ml of fresh water and turn off heat.

Cook the pasta in the salted boiling water until it's a minute or so away from al dente, about 3 minutes, then drain the pasta well.

Turn the heat under the frying pan to high and let the liquid come to

*serves 4 to 6 as a main*

Sea salt

450g fresh golden girolles, cleaned (see 'Cleaning Wild Mushrooms', opposite)

2 tablespoons extra-virgin olive oil

2 medium garlic cloves, thinly sliced

6 tablespoons unsalted butter, cut into several pieces

Maldon or another flaky sea salt

Fresh Egg Pasta (page 127), cut into pappardelle

2 teaspoons lemon juice, plus more to taste

A small handful of delicate flat-leaf parsley sprigs, roughly chopped

A handful of finely grated Parmesan cheese

a vigorous simmer. Add the pasta, lemon juice and parsley, toss well and cook, tossing occasionally, until the pasta is al dente and the liquid has evaporated but the pasta still looks glossy, 1 to 2 minutes. Season to taste with salt and just enough lemon juice to add brightness, not acidity. Divide among plates, sprinkle on the Parmesan and serve straightaway.

## CLEANING WILD MUSHROOMS

To clean the mushrooms, cut away any brown bits from the bottom of the stems. Fill a big bowl with water, add the mushrooms and use your hands to gently submerge them in the water and agitate them a bit, rubbing them gently if the visible dirt is particularly stubborn. Do not keep the mushrooms in the water for more than 20 seconds or so. Transfer to kitchen paper to drain and pat dry.

# SWISS CHARD CANNELLONI

All you need for a winter dinner party are these trays of cannelloni filled with velvety, lemony chard. Add a big old salad of bitter greens and everyone's happy. Instead of the typical lake of béchamel sauce that often drowns cannelloni, I prefer using a lighter hand with a more delicate mixture of cream, milk and lemon zest. Otherwise, the dish would be too heavy and less about the fresh pasta and the chard. As it all bakes, the little pools of cream thicken and go golden at the edges, and the tops of the pasta tubes get a bit bubbly and crispy.

Ready a large bowl of icy water. Grab a few clean kitchen towels, get them damp, and lay out one on a work surface.

Bring a large pot of water to a boil and add enough sea salt so it tastes lightly salty. Cook the pasta in batches, 6 or so sheets at a time, in the boiling water for 1 minute, and transfer the sheets as they're done to the icy water, using your hands to help them lay flat (not folded or doubled over) in the water.

Lay as many rectangles of pasta on the towel as will fit in one layer, cover them with another towel, and repeat until they're all laid out and covered.

Combine the chard in a bowl with the ricotta, a quarter of the Parmesan, the egg, 2 teaspoons of the Maldon salt, and pepper to taste, and stir really well.

Lightly coat the bottoms and sides of 2 large, heavy enamelled baking dishes with olive oil (about 1 tablespoon per dish).

Grab a rectangle of pasta, lay it on your work surface, and spread about 1½ tablespoons of the chard mixture along one of the short sides, leaving a bit of space at the edges. Starting from the side with the filling, roll the rectangle over the filling into a neat cylinder, transfer it to one of the baking dishes, and repeat with the rest of the filling and pasta. It's fine if not all of the cylinders line up the same

SPECIAL EQUIPMENT
2 large, heavy enamelled baking dishes (each about 25 x 36cm)

Sea salt

Fresh Egg Pasta (page 127), prepped for cannelloni

Swiss Chard (Leaves and Stems) with Marjoram (page 75), at room temperature

450g ricotta

50g Parmesan cheese, finely grated

1 large egg, lightly beaten

3 teaspoons Maldon or another flaky sea salt

Freshly ground black pepper

6 tablespoons extra-virgin olive oil

4 medium garlic cloves, thinly sliced

480ml double cream

225ml whole milk

½ teaspoon packed finely grated lemon zest

A five-finger pinch of basil leaves

A five-finger pinch of tender fennel fronds

way in the pan. Drizzle about 1 tablespoon of olive oil over each baking dish.

Position a rack in the centre of the oven and preheat to 230°C/gas 8.

Heat the remaining 2 tablespoons of oil in a large cast-iron frying pan over high heat until it shimmers. Add the garlic and cook, stirring frequently, until the garlic is light golden brown and smells toasty, 30 seconds to 1 minute. Add the cream, milk, lemon zest, and remaining 1 teaspoon of Maldon salt to the frying pan. Let the mixture come to a full boil, then pour it evenly over the cannelloni. I like to leave the parts of the cannelloni at the edges of the dish unsauced, so they get a bit crispy later during baking. Sprinkle two-thirds of the remaining Parmesan over the cannelloni.

Bake the cannelloni until it has brown patches on top and the sauce at the edge of the dishes has gone golden brown, about 20 minutes.

Roughly chop the basil and fennel fronds and sprinkle them over the cannelloni along with the last of the Parmesan. Serve straightaway.

# LUMACONI STUFFED WITH SUMMER VEGETABLES

Lumaconi is dried pasta in the shape of a big snail shell that just begs to be stuffed. I often fantasise about what I can stuff them with. The first time I ate lumaconi, they were filled with sausage. The first time I made them, it was springtime, and I filled the shells with Jerusalem artichokes, peas and tomatoes. This recipe is for summer, a sort of succotash in pasta form. Into each shell, you spoon a simple stew of tomatoes, corn, courgette and green beans, which gets some meaty complexity from slow-cooked red onion and garlic. Pour on a little cream and into the oven goes the pasta to get a bit toasty and crispy.

Bring a large pot of water to a boil. Fill a big bowl with icy water. Add the tomatoes to the boiling water, wait 15 seconds (or 30 seconds if you've got especially firm tomatoes), then use a spider to gently transfer them to the icy water. Be sure to keep the water in the pot at a boil.

Peel the tomatoes, discarding the skins, and set them aside.

Refill the big bowl with cold water. Generously salt the boiling water until it tastes a little less salty than the sea. Add the pasta and cook according to instructions on the package until al dente, about 9 minutes. Drain well, put the pasta in the bowl of cold water and let the pasta sit just until it's fully cool. Transfer the pasta opening side down to a plate lined with kitchen paper to drain.

Cut the corn kernels from the ears, then use the back of your knife to scrape each cob to get at any bits of kernel left behind. Combine the kernels and scrapings in a bowl. Cut the cobs into a few pieces and pop them into a medium pot along with the cream and ½ teaspoon of the Maldon salt. Bring the cream to a boil over high heat, then remove the pot from the heat.

Rinse and wipe the large pot. Pour in the oil and set the pot over medium-high heat until the oil shimmers. Add the onion and 1

**serves 4 to 6 as a main**

775g cherry tomatoes, each pricked with the tip of a sharp knife

Sea salt

250g dried lumaconi pasta (about 30) or jumbo shell pasta

2 large ears corn, shucked

600ml double cream

2½ teaspoons Maldon or another flaky sea salt

55ml extra-virgin olive oil

1 medium-large red onion (about 330g), halved lengthwise and thinly sliced

3 medium garlic cloves, thinly sliced

A small handful of basil leaves, roughly chopped at the last minute

3 dried pequín chillies, crumbled, or pinches of red pepper flakes

225g courgettes, topped, tailed and cut into 1-cm irregularly shaped pieces

150g green beans, topped, tailed and cut into 2.5-cm pieces

A handful of finely grated Parmesan cheese

teaspoon of the Maldon salt and cook, stirring occasionally until wilted, about 5 minutes. Push the onion to the side, add the garlic to the slick of oil and cook until it's toasty and turns a light golden colour, 1 to 2 minutes. Give it all a good stir, cover, reduce the heat to medium-low and cook until the onions are very soft, about 10 minutes. Stir in half the basil and cook, uncovered, stirring occasionally until the onions are lightly browned, about 8 minutes more.

Add the tomatoes and the remaining 1 teaspoon of the Maldon salt to the pot and cook, stirring and mashing the tomatoes until they've released their liquid and are almost completely broken down, about 12 minutes. Add the corn, increase the heat to bring the mixture to a strong simmer and cook until the kernels are tender but still have a pop, about 5 minutes. Add the chillies, courgette, green beans and the remaining basil, and cook at a strong simmer, stirring, until the courgette and green beans are tender with a slight snap, 5 to 8 minutes. Remove the vegetables from the heat.

Position a rack in the centre of the oven and preheat to 200°C/gas 6.

Grab a heavy enamelled baking dish large enough to fit the lumaconi in a single layer with a little room to spare. Fill each noodle with about 2 tablespoons of the vegetable mixture and add them opening side up to the baking dish.

Discard the corncobs, then pour the cream evenly over the stuffed lumaconi. Bake until the cream has thickened and turned light golden at the edges of the dish, about 20 minutes. Sprinkle on the Parmesan, turn on the grill and cook just until the cheese has turned light golden brown in spots, 3 to 5 minutes more. Let the dish cool just slightly and serve.

# KALE POLENTA

In the US, polenta is typically served as a side dish. But in Italy, it is often the main attraction – a real showstopper. I've been seated at a table with friends when the cook arrived from the kitchen with the pot of polenta. Instead of ladling the polenta onto our empty plates, as I first expected, the cook poured the polenta from the pot straight onto a wooden board in the centre of the table. Steamy and inviting, it crept outward like hot lava.

My Kale Polenta is a showstopper in its own right: its striking green colour is beautiful and unexpected. It's so stunning you can skip the board and just haul the pot to the table. The healthy dose of kale purée that colours the cornmeal adds lots of flavour, too. You taste the sweetness of the corn polenta first, then a hint of garlic, and finally that green minerality of kale at the end.

Combine 1.5 litres of water and the salt in a medium pot and bring the water to a boil over high heat. Gradually add the polenta, whisking as you pour. Keep whisking until the polenta starts to thicken and looks like it's one with the water, about 2 minutes. Turn the heat to low (the polenta should steam and tremble, but only rarely erupt with bubbles) and cook, stirring every now and again, until the polenta is tender but still slightly coarse in texture, about 45 minutes.

Stir in the olive oil, kale purée and most of the Parmesan, and keep cooking, stirring occasionally, for a few minutes more. Take the pot off the heat and fold in 2 tablespoons of the mascarpone (it's nice to run into a little pocket of mascarpone, so don't stir too much). Top with the remaining mascarpone and Parmesan, and as much black pepper as you'd like.

serves 6 to 8 as a side

330g coarse stone-ground polenta

55ml extra-virgin olive oil

110g Kale Purée (page 235)

50g Parmesan cheese, finely grated

3 tablespoons mascarpone

1 tablespoon plus 1 teaspoon Maldon or another flaky sea salt

Coarsely ground black pepper

# SWEET-CORN POLENTA

When you can get your mitts on high-quality stone-ground stuff, polenta becomes more than just a vehicle for butter and Parmesan. Great polenta has character – a pleasantly coarse texture and the unmistakable flavour of corn. I like to add summer's finest fresh corn, with the soft crunch of its kernels and its unparalleled sweetness, to underscore the polenta's flavour and contrast its texture.

Cut the corn kernels from the cobs, then use the back of the knife to scrape each cob to get at any bits of kernel left behind. Combine the kernels and scrapings in a bowl, and reserve the cobs.

Cut the cobs crosswise into a few pieces, combine them with 1.5 litres of water in a medium pot, and cover the pot. Bring the water to a boil over high heat, then uncover the pot and remove and discard the cobs.

Stir in the salt, then gradually add the polenta, whisking as you pour. Keep whisking until the polenta starts to thicken and looks like it's one with the water, about 2 minutes. Turn the heat to low (the polenta should steam and tremble, but only rarely erupt with bubbles) and cook, stirring every now and again, for 20 minutes. Stir in the corn kernels and scrapings and continue to cook the polenta until it's tender but still slightly coarse in texture, about 25 minutes more.

Take the pot off the heat, stir in the butter and most of the Parmesan, then season with salt to taste. Sprinkle on the remaining Parmesan and as much black pepper as you'd like.

serves 6 to 8 as a side

4 medium ears corn, shucked

1 tablespoon plus 1 teaspoon Maldon or another flaky sea salt

330g coarse stone-ground polenta

3 tablespoons unsalted butter

50g Parmesan cheese, finely grated

Coarsely ground black pepper

# BUTTERNUT SQUASH POLENTA

There are earthy, creamy chunks of winter squash lurking in this pot of polenta. I stir in the squash roughly, so it's not entirely incorporated and some stays in larger pieces. That way, each bite is different. And I love getting a sneaky hit of heat from the chilli. You can roast the squash as the polenta bubbles, which means this dish takes only slightly more effort and almost no extra time than plain old polenta.

serves 6 to 8 as a side

1 tablespoon plus
3 teaspoons Maldon or another flaky sea salt

330g coarse stone-ground polenta

900g butternut squash, peeled, seeded and cut into irregular 5-cm chunks

55ml plus 2 tablespoons extra-virgin olive oil

2 medium garlic cloves, finely chopped and smooshed to a paste

3 dried pequín chillies, crumbled, or pinches of red pepper flakes

2 tablespoons unsalted butter

50g Parmesan cheese, finely grated

3 tablespoons mascarpone

Coarsely ground black pepper

Position a rack in the centre of the oven and preheat to its highest setting.

Combine 1.5 litres of water and 1 tablespoon plus 1 teaspoon of the salt in a medium pot and bring the water to a boil over high heat. Gradually add the polenta, whisking as you pour. Keep whisking until the polenta starts to thicken and looks like it's one with the water, about 2 minutes. Turn down the heat to low (the polenta should steam and tremble, but only rarely erupt with bubbles) and cook, stirring every now and again, until the polenta is tender but still slightly coarse in texture, about 45 minutes. Cover and keep the polenta warm over very low heat.

Meanwhile, toss the squash with 55ml of the oil, the garlic, the remaining 2 teaspoons of salt and the chillies in a heavy enamelled baking dish large enough to fit the squash in a single layer with a little room to spare. Pour 110ml of water into the pan (around but not over the squash), cover the pan tightly with foil, and bake until the squash is fork-tender, 30 to 40 minutes. Remove the foil and bake until the squash is very tender but not mushy and the bottoms have browned a bit, about 15 minutes more.

Add the squash, including any bits stuck to the pan, to the polenta and have at it with a whisk, stirring and smashing so some of the squash is incorporated into the polenta and some remains in chunks.

Stir in the remaining 2 tablespoons of oil, the butter and most of the Parmesan. Take the pot off the heat and fold in 2 tablespoons of the mascarpone (it's nice to run into a little pocket of mascarpone, so don't stir too much). Top with the remaining mascarpone and Parmesan, and as much black pepper as you'd like.

# FOCACCIA

I know good focaccia when I put a knife through it – when the blade cracks through the crust with a crunch, and I can't help but smile. That crunch and an airy crumb tell me right away that I'm not about to eat one of those dense, dry versions that have threatened to tarnish the bread's reputation. Although the best breads often come from great bakeries, where the people running the place have spent years perfecting their craft, focaccia is one of those relatively simple breads that home cooks can manage. This recipe is based on Nancy Silverton's, because she's just brilliant. The neat part about making focaccia yourself is not just that you get to eat it when it's good and fresh, but that you get to experience all the little joyous moments along the way, like when your *biga* (the starter) develops happy bubbles and when the dough becomes elastic and smooth as a baby's bum. Focaccia makes a delicious vehicle for vegetables, too. I provide two options of toppings – one with butternut squash and another with thinly sliced potatoes – but I hope you'll have fun coming up with your own.

## make the biga

About twenty-four hours before you plan to bake the focaccia: combine the tepid water and yeast in a small bowl and stir with a wooden spoon until the yeast has dissolved, 30 seconds or so. Put the bread flour in a medium bowl, pour in the yeast mixture and stir until the flour is incorporated and the ingredients are well combined.

Cover the bowl tightly with clingfilm and leave in a warm place until the mixture looks bubbly and has thickened (when you tip the bowl it should just barely creep forward), 18 to 24 hours.

## make the dough

A few hours before you plan to bake the focaccia, combine the yeast, bread flour, 1 tablespoon of the oil, 280ml of water and all of the biga in the bowl of a stand mixer fitted with a dough hook. Mix on low speed until you have a uniform dough (about 1 minute), then increase the speed to medium, slowly sprinkle in the salt and mix, stopping to

### makes two 20-cm rounds

**SPECIAL EQUIPMENT**

A stand mixer with dough hook attachment and two 20-cm round cake tins (5cm deep)

**FOR THE BIGA**

About 100ml tepid water

Scant ⅛ teaspoon packed cake yeast or scant ¹⁄₁₆ teaspoon active dry yeast (not instant or rapid-rise)

100g bread flour

**FOR THE DOUGH**

34g fresh cake yeast, crumbled, or 17g active dry yeast (not instant or rapid-rise)

475g bread flour, plus a little extra as needed

1 tablespoon extra-virgin olive oil, plus a glug for coating the bowl

1 tablespoon sea salt

scrape down the sides of the bowl if need be, just until the dough is smooth and elastic and it begins to pull away from and slap against the bowl of the mixer, 6 to 8 minutes. If the dough is too moist, it won't pull away from the bowl so, if need be, gradually add a little more flour. If the dough is too dry, it won't be smooth so, if need be, gradually add a little more water.

Turn the dough onto a lightly floured surface and use your hands to make sure the ball of dough is nice and round.

Add a glug of olive oil to a bowl large enough to hold at least twice the amount of dough, then wipe the bowl with a piece of kitchen paper to coat it with a thin layer of the oil. Add the dough, cover the bowl tightly with clingfilm, and put it in a warm place until it has doubled in size, 1 to 1½ hours.

**top and bake the focaccia**
While the dough is doubling, make the topping of choice.

Pour 55ml of the oil into two 20-cm round cake tins and tilt them so the oil covers the surfaces.

FOR TOPPING AND BAKING

Butternut, Sage and Chillies (page 151) or Potatoes, Red Onion and Thyme (page 152)

55ml extra-virgin olive oil, plus a glug for baking

Turn the dough onto a lightly floured surface and cut it in half. (I like to be precise and weigh the dough. You'll have about 900g, and each half should weigh about 450g.) Add a half to each cake tin and use your fingers to gently pull the edges of the dough towards the sides of each tin. Cover the tins tightly with clingfilm and put them in a warm place until the dough relaxes and has puffed up a little, about 25 minutes.

Spread the topping evenly onto the dough, leaving about a 2.5cm border. Press down lightly so the topping sinks in slightly, and gently push the edges so they more or less reach the sides of the cake tin. Cover with clingfilm again and let it puff up a little more, 15 to 30 minutes.

Position a rack in the centre of the oven and preheat to its highest setting. Drizzle on a little more olive oil (about 1 tablespoon), put the focaccia on the centre rack and bake, rotating the tins once, until the crust and undersides (use a spatula to have a peek) are light golden brown, about 25 minutes.

Transfer the tins to a rack to cool slightly, then slice however you wish and eat the focaccia warm or at room temperature.

# BUTTERNUT, SAGE AND CHILLIES

3 tablespoons extra-virgin olive oil, plus a healthy drizzle for finishing

675g butternut squash, peeled, seeded and cut into 1-cm cubes

6 medium garlic cloves, thinly sliced

5 or so dried pequín chillies, crumbled, or pinches of red pepper flakes

A small handful of sage leaves, torn if large

1½ teaspoons plus a healthy pinch Maldon or another flaky sea salt

15g aged pecorino cheese (preferably pecorino ginepro), finely grated

While the focaccia dough is doubling, make the topping. Heat the oil in a medium cast-iron frying pan over medium-high heat until it smokes lightly. Add the squash (it's OK if it's not in one layer) and cook, stirring and tossing occasionally, just until the edges begin to brown, 5 to 7 minutes. The squash cubes will still be slightly crunchy in the middle.

Push the squash to one side of the frying pan. Add the garlic to the empty side and sprinkle the chillies over the squash. Cook the garlic, stirring until it's golden brown at the edges, about 1 minute, then mix everything together. Cook for a minute more, add the sage and 1½ teaspoons of Maldon salt, and remove the pan from the heat. Stir well and let the mixture cool.

Top and bake the focaccia as directed (page 149). After removing the focaccia from the oven, sprinkle them with a healthy pinch of Maldon salt, add a healthy drizzle of olive oil (2 to 3 tablespoons) to the topping and crust, and sprinkle on the pecorino.

# POTATOES, RED ONION AND THYME

**enough for two 20-cm focaccia**

150g waxy baby potatoes, unpeeled

2 medium garlic cloves, finely grated

3 tablespoons extra-virgin olive oil

1½ teaspoons Maldon or another flaky sea salt

1 small red onion (a generous 110g), halved lengthwise and thinly sliced

2 tablespoons packed pitted, roughly chopped Niçoise or Taggiasca olives

A five-finger pinch of thyme leaves, coarsely chopped

A few splashes of red wine vinegar

While the focaccia dough is doubling, make the topping. Use a vegetable peeler to shave the potatoes lengthwise into irregular thin slices. As you work, immediately put the slices in a medium mixing bowl with 2 tablespoons of the oil (to prevent browning) and toss well. Add the onion, thyme and garlic, and toss well. Top and bake the focaccia as directed (page 149), sprinkling on the salt just before you pop the tins in the oven.

Meanwhile, stir together the olives, the remaining 1 tablespoon of oil and the vinegar. After removing the focaccia from the oven, spoon the olive mixture here and there on top of the focaccia and serve.

# MUSHROOM PIES WITH SWISS CHARD

There's a football chant used to taunt players who look less than fit on the field. 'Who ate all the pies?' your team's fans all ask at once, before everyone answers, 'You fat bastard, you fat bastard!' Of course, the fans aren't talking about blueberry or cherry pie; the British use of the word refers first and foremost to all manner of savoury filled pastries (though a few pies, like shepherd's, have no pastry at all). There's steak and kidney pie, beef and Stilton pie, and pork pie, the latter so famous someone named a hat after it. In Cornwall, you'll find stargazy pie, which features sardine-like fish with their heads poking out of the top crust as if they were gazing at the stars. There are too many pies to list them all. The point is that they're so common and so beloved that, to fans, pies are the inevitable culprit behind lethargic footballers.

I too remember feeling a bit sluggish after taking down a chicken and mushroom pie at the pub or chippy. While you wouldn't want a pie to be light – then it'd no longer be a pie, would it? – I do think of this version as a little more elegant than my girlhood favourites. I leave out the meat altogether, opting instead for mushrooms (sturdy, common ones for bulk and texture, and wild ones for flavour) with a touch of cream for richness. I add chard, because I like the way its lemony quality brightens the pie. Each pie is an ample dinner with a simple salad.

## make the dough

Combine the flour, sugar, and salt in a large mixing bowl and stir very well. Add the butter to the flour mixture and toss to coat with flour. Then work swiftly (the last thing you want is for the butter to melt) to break up and smoosh the butter lumps with your fingertips just until none are much bigger than peas.

Pour in the buttermilk and water, stir well with a fork, then use your hands to swiftly scrunch and pack (don't knead) the mixture just until it comes together into a blob. If there's lots of loose flour, gradually add more water, then scrunch and pack again. Cut the dough in half, wrap each half in clingfilm and refrigerate the dough for at least 1 hour or up to 12 hours.

makes four 12-cm pies

SPECIAL EQUIPMENT
4 nonstick mini (12cm) pie tins

FOR THE DOUGH
285g plain flour

1 tablespoon granulated sugar

1 teaspoon sea salt

225g very cold unsalted butter, cut into 1-cm pieces just before using

110ml cold, well-shaken buttermilk

1 tablespoon cold water, or more if necessary

FOR THE FILLING
50g unsalted butter

1 medium Spanish onion (about 225g), thinly sliced

2 medium garlic cloves, thinly sliced

1 tablespoon thyme leaves, roughly chopped

2 teaspoons Maldon or another flaky sea salt

(continued on next page)

**153**

### make the filling

Melt the butter in a medium pot over medium heat. Add the onion, garlic, thyme, and 1 teaspoon of the Maldon salt and cook, stirring occasionally, until the onion is very soft with just a kiss of brown, about 20 minutes. Use a slotted spoon to transfer the mixture to a bowl, leaving the butter behind.

Increase the heat to medium-high, add the chard stems to the pot and cook, stirring and scraping the pot, until they're lightly browned at the edges, about 5 minutes. Add the mushrooms to the pot and cook, stirring almost constantly for a minute. Add the onion mixture and the remaining 1 teaspoon of salt. Cook, stirring and scraping often, until the mushrooms are just cooked through and the chard stems are tender with a slight crunch, about 5 minutes. Pour in the cream, let it come to a boil, then remove the pot from the heat. Let the mixture cool completely. You can make this up to a day in advance.

Pour just enough water into a large cast-iron frying pan with a lid to barely cover its surface. Bring the water to a boil, add the chard leaves and pop on the lid. Cook, stirring once, until the leaves are fully wilted and tender, about 3 minutes. Drain the chard, let it cool to the touch and squeeze out as much liquid as you can. Give the leaves a rough chop and stir them into the mushroom mixture.

### make and bake the pies

Position a rack in the centre of the oven and preheat to 190°C/gas 5.

Take one of the dough halves from the fridge and cut it into 4 equal pieces. Lightly flour your work surface. Working with one piece at a time (and keeping the others, covered, in the fridge), roll the dough into a rough 18-cm round that's about 3mm thick. Lay it in one of the pie tins, gently pressing it against the bottom and up the sides so it fits securely. Use a knife to trim off the overhang and then put the pie shell in the fridge while you roll out the three remaining pieces. Chill the shells in the fridge for 30 minutes or so.

450g green Swiss chard, stems trimmed and cut on the diagonal into 1-cm wide slices, leaves torn in half

175g mixed wild mushrooms, separated or cut into about 4 x 1cm pieces

100g portobello caps, peeled and cut into irregular pieces about as large as the other mushrooms

240ml double cream

4 teaspoons crème fraîche

1 large egg yolk

1 tablespoon whole milk

Cut four 15-cm squares of baking parchment. Crumple each square into a ball, wet the ball under running water, squeeze out all the water, then flatten out the squares again. (This makes them more malleable.) Line each pie shell with a piece of baking parchment and fill it with uncooked rice or dried beans, using your fingers to make sure the rice or beans go all the way to the edges. Put the pie tins on a baking sheet and bake, rotating the baking sheet once, just until the rim of the dough no longer looks raw, about 15 minutes.

Take the pans out of the oven, wait 5 minutes or so, then carefully remove the paper and rice or beans. (You can save the rice or beans to use the next time you bake.) Divide the filling among the 4 crusts and add 1 teaspoon of crème fraîche to the centre of each pie.

Whisk together the egg yolk and milk in a small bowl. Brush the rim of the crusts with some of the egg mixture. Take the remaining dough from the fridge and cut it into 4 equal pieces. Working with one piece at a time (and that's keeping the remaining pieces covered in the fridge), roll into an 18-cm round about 3mm thick, lay the rounds over each pie and press them lightly against the edge of the crust so they adhere. Trim off any overhang with a knife and crimp the edges of the pie. Brush the tops with the egg mixture, return the pies to the baking sheet and bake them, rotating the sheet occasionally, until the tops are golden brown, about 35 minutes.

Carefully invert each dish; the pie should slip right out. If not, use a knife to make sure the edges have separated from the tin. Serve them tops-up on plates and eat straightaway.

# BUTTERNUT SQUASH-COCONUT TART

My first Thanksgiving, when I had my first taste of pumpkin pie, was fairly typical – you know, just me sitting at a long table with Mario Batali and his family. I was fresh off the boat from London, just after I became the chef of the Spotted Pig. I didn't know anyone in New York and Mario was kind enough to invite me to share his holiday meal. I remember being quite nervous, because I'd made a pumpkin caponata (a sort of sweet-sour savoury relish typically made from aubergine) and I hoped Mario would like it. Someone had brought a pumpkin pie, which I had assumed, being from the land of meat pies, would be a savoury dish as well. I was surprised when it came out for dessert. Yet I adored it. Pumpkin – as well as winter squashes like butternut – is one of those vegetables that's as at home during dinner as it is after. So long as there's not too much spice getting in the way of the earthy, melony squash flavour, I'm a big fan. This is my favourite version, with a sneaky bit of coconut milk providing richness and a compelling something special that your mates will love, even if they can't quite identify the source. A good dollop of whipped cream and a sprinkle of toasted coconut flakes make a nice topping.

## make the tart shell

Sift the flour into the food processor, then add the icing sugar, butter and salt. Pulse the mixture until it looks like fine breadcrumbs. Add the egg yolks and pulse until a crumbly dough forms. Scrape the dough out onto a work surface and lightly knead just until smooth. Form the dough into a ball, wrap it in clingfilm and refrigerate it for at least 1 hour or up to 2 days.

Position a rack in the centre of the oven and preheat to 180°C/gas 4.

Cut the chilled dough into 2 or 3 large pieces and grate it through the large holes of a box grater. Use your fingers to press the dough onto the bottom and up the sides of the pie dish to create an even layer that's about 0.5cm thick on the sides and 8mm thick on the bottom. (If you're using the 22-cm pie dish, you'll have enough dough and

**makes one
23-cm tart**

SPECIAL EQUIPMENT

A heavy 25cm fluted pie dish (about 7cm deep) or a heavy 22cm dish (about 5cm deep)

FOR THE TART SHELL

280g plain flour

90g icing sugar

150g cold unsalted butter, cut into 0.5-cm pieces

¼ teaspoon plus ⅛ teaspoon sea salt

3 large egg yolks, lightly beaten

FOR THE FILLING

A 1.3kg butternut squash, peeled and cut into 2.5-cm cubes

335ml well-stirred tinned unsweetened coconut milk

225g caster sugar

⅛ teaspoon ground cinnamon

5 large eggs plus 1 egg yolk

filling left over to make a mini pie, a special treat for the cook.) Work swiftly – you don't want the dough to warm up too much. Gently prick the bottom here and there with a fork, which will prevent it from puffing up as it bakes, then pop the dish into the freezer for 15 minutes.

Cut out a 30-cm round of baking parchment and line the dough with it. Fill the tart shell with uncooked rice or dried beans, using your fingers to make sure the rice or beans go all the way to the edge. Put the tart shell on a baking sheet and bake just until the rim begins to turn light golden brown, about 15 minutes. Carefully remove the paper and rice or beans. Let the shell cool while you make the filling. Keep the oven on.

### make the filling

Put the squash in a heavy enamelled baking dish in a single layer, cover the dish tightly with foil and bake, stirring once and re-covering tightly with foil, until the squash is very soft, about 55 minutes. Leave the oven on.

Transfer the squash to a blender. Add the coconut milk and purée until very smooth. With the blender running on low, add the sugar, cinnamon and, one at a time, the whole eggs and the egg yolk. Keep the blender running just until the eggs are fully incorporated into the mixture.

Put the tart shell on a baking sheet. Pour just enough of the squash mixture into the tart shell to come up to about 1cm from the rim, reserving the rest for the mini pie. Bake, rotating the pan once, until the crust is golden brown and the filling has just set, 45 minutes to 1 hour. After about 30 minutes, take a peek at the exposed crust. If it already looks light golden brown, carefully cover the exposed crust with foil for the remainder of the baking time.

Remove the pan from the oven and let the tart cool to room temperature before slicing. It keeps covered in the fridge for up to a day or two.

# BROCCOLI RAAB MORNING BUNS

If you've never heard of a morning bun, your first order of business should be popping over to San Francisco and heading to Tartine Bakery. Behind the glass of the display case, you'll spot spiral-shaped little pillows baked with orange-cinnamon sugar, the centre of each one rising up like a hill. That is, if you haven't arrived too late. They're magic, really – buttery layers of dough that are somehow both rich and delicate, crackly on the outsides and soft in the middle. Whenever I cook them, they get me thinking. As a cook obsessed with Italian food, the orange element brings to mind rosemary (the two often join forces in Sicily), which brings to mind all sorts of savoury, Italianesque options, like this version laced with pesto made from pleasantly bitter raab and musty, sharp aged provolone.

## make the yeast dough

Combine 220ml of the warm milk and the yeast in a small mixing bowl and stir with a wooden spoon until the yeast has mostly dissolved. Let the mixture sit until the surface bubbles, about 5 minutes.

In the bowl of a stand mixer fitted with the dough hook, stir together the flour, sugar and salt. Add the yeast-milk mixture, then swish the remaining 55ml of warm milk in the small bowl to get at any yeast left behind and pour it into the bowl of the stand mixer. Mix on low speed for 2 minutes. If there's still loose flour visible after the dough forms, gradually add up to 2 tablespoons more warm milk until all of the flour is incorporated.

Increase the speed to medium-low (if your mixer is struggling a bit, take out the dough, cut it in half and work one piece at a time) until the dough is smooth and slightly tacky, 3 to 4 minutes.

Add a glug of oil to a bowl large enough to hold at least twice the amount of dough, then wipe the bowl with kitchen paper to coat it with a thin layer of the oil. Add the dough, cover the bowl tightly with clingfilm and leave it at room temperature until it has increased in size 1½ to 2 times, 30 minutes to 1 hour. Put it in the fridge overnight.

**makes 12 buns**

### SPECIAL EQUIPMENT

A stand mixer with dough hook and paddle attachments, two 1.5-litre jumbo muffin tins, and a rolling pin

### FOR THE YEAST DOUGH

275ml whole milk, gently heated just until warm to the touch, plus 2 tablespoons as needed

25g cake yeast, crumbled, or 1 tablespoon plus 1 teaspoon active dry yeast (not instant or rapid-rise)

500g plain flour

2 tablespoons granulated sugar

2 teaspoons sea salt

A glug of neutral oil, such as rapeseed

### FOR THE BUTTER BLOB

450g cold unsalted butter, cut into about 1-cm slices

2 tablespoons plain flour

## make the butter blob

Wash the bowl of the stand mixer and fit the mixer with the paddle attachment. Combine the butter and flour in the bowl. Mix at low speed for 10 seconds or so, then at medium speed until the butter and flour are well combined and there are no lumps but not so long that the butter is no longer cold, about 1 minute. Transfer the blob to a clean surface and work swiftly to shape it into a 17 x 15cm rectangle. Wrap it in clingfilm and pop it in the fridge until it's well chilled, at least 8 hours or overnight.

## make the morning bun dough

Take the butter blob from the fridge and let it sit at room temperature for a minute or two just to take the chill off. Do not let it get warm. Put the yeast dough on a clean, lightly floured surface and use a heavy rolling pin to roll it into a rough 40 x 20cm rectangle. Position the dough so a long side faces you. Put the butter blob in the centre of the dough so its slightly shorter side faces you. Fold one of the dough's short sides over the butter so it just covers half of the butter. Fold the opposite side so it covers the other half of the butter. Gently pinch together the dough edges at the centre to seal in the butter.

Roll from short end to short end, flipping over the dough once and dusting it and the work surface with flour so it won't stick to the pin or surface, until you have an even rectangle that's about 55 x 22cm. (To achieve the 23-cm width, you might have to rotate the dough 90 degrees and roll briefly.)

Fold the dough into thirds as though it were a letter, gently wiping away the excess flour on the top and bottom of the dough as you do. Start by folding one of the short sides to create an approximately 38 x 22cm rectangle, then fold the other short side to create an approximately 20 x 22cm rectangle. Wrap the dough in plastic wrap and refrigerate for 1 hour. You're going to repeat this process three more times, so each time, scribble down a number to keep track of how many you've completed.

FOR THE PESTO FILLING

350g lightly packed roughly chopped broccoli raab (stalks that are 0.5cm or thinner, leaves and florets)

3 medium garlic cloves, roughly chopped

125g aged provolone, roughly chopped

3 tablespoons extra-virgin olive oil

1 teaspoon crumbled dried pequín chillies, or pinches of red pepper flakes

1 tablespoon Maldon or another flaky sea salt

Wait a few minutes until the chill comes off the dough so it's easier to roll, but don't let it get warm. Position the dough so that the rounded side faces your left. Then gently roll the dough into an even rectangle that's about 55 x 22cm. For the second time, fold the dough into thirds as though it were a letter. Wrap the dough in plastic wrap and refrigerate for 1 hour. Repeat the process – rolling, folding and refrigerating – twice more.

### meanwhile, make the pesto filling

Working in batches if necessary, combine the broccoli raab and garlic in a food processor and pulse, stirring occasionally, until the raab is finely chopped and there are no large pieces of garlic. Transfer the mixture to a mixing bowl. Add the provolone to the processor and pulse until it's in small chunks, then transfer it to the bowl. Add the oil, chillies and salt, and stir well.

### bake the buns

Roll the dough out to an even 45 x 30cm rectangle.

Spread the pesto evenly onto the dough, leaving a 1cm border on all sides. Use your hands to roll up the dough to form a tight 45-cm long log. Run wet fingers along the seam, then turn the log seam-side down and press down gently so the seam adheres.

Cut the log crosswise into twelve 4-cm thick pieces. Put the slices into the cups of the jumbo muffin tins and lightly press down so they touch the bottoms of the cups. Cover them loosely with clingfilm (or even better, use an overturned clean plastic tub to avoid the risk of the clingfilm sticking after the dough rises) and keep them in a warm place until the dough rises a bit above the rim, about 1 hour.

Meanwhile, position a rack in the centre of the oven and preheat to 240°C/gas 9. Bake the buns on the rack (if both muffin tins can't fit on the centre rack, bake in two batches) until they're croissant-golden-brown and crispy, 12 to 15 minutes. Carefully prise them out of the muffin tins and let them cool slightly on a wire rack.

## simple things
# broccoli raab

Sweetness is easy to love. Too easy. I think that's why I love bitter vegetables so much: because loving them requires a little effort. Take broccoli raab. When I was a girl, I would never have chosen the slightly acrid, minerally green vegetable over peas, let alone a Cadbury Creme Egg or a Curly Wurly. And even though our taste buds change as we get older, I didn't wake up one day and suddenly crave broccoli raab. The appreciation came slowly. I had to eat it again and again before I turned the corner. That's very adult, isn't it? To realise that the people and things and pleasures that are worth one's while take work.

So I say, seek out broccoli raab that has a real bite. Have a nibble of a raw leaf and make sure its bitterness is intense, that it makes you perk up as it catches the back of your tongue. At home, I'll often do little more than sauté broccoli raab with garlic, salt and chilli, which provide balance that lets you enjoy the bitterness. Trim off any brown or woody bottoms, then get a few good glugs of olive oil hot in a heavy cast-iron frying pan. Add a few thinly sliced garlic cloves and move them around, watching as they get golden brown and toasty. Crumble in a bit of chilli, then add your raab, making sure not to crowd the pan, or else it'll steam. Cook, tossing occasionally, until the raab stems are tender with a slight snap. Sometimes I like when the raab has just a kiss of brown. Sometimes I increase the heat so the raab goes all wilty and crispy. Sprinkle on some flaky sea salt and have another toss. With vegetables this bitter, life sure is sweet.

a little beast
goes a long way

# SWEET POTATOES WITH BONE MARROW, CHILLI AND MAPLE SYRUP

My mate Fergus Henderson has long celebrated the glories of marrow at his restaurants, where he roasts veal shank bones until the marrow inside is wiggly, perfect for scooping out and spreading onto bread. I also use marrow as if it were beefy butter, though in this dish I go a different route: the bones roast along *with* the sweet potatoes. The marrow melts into the pan, soaking into the potatoes, helping them go brown and crispy.

Position a rack in the centre of the oven and preheat to 230°C/gas 8.

Put the potato rounds in a medium pot, pour in just enough water to cover them by about 1cm and add the sea salt. Bring the water to a boil over high heat, lower the heat to maintain a strong simmer, and cook the potatoes just until they're fully tender (a knife will meet the slightest resistance in the centre of each slice), 15 to 20 minutes. Drain them well and let them sit uncovered in the colander for about 15 minutes.

Put the rounds flat on your work surface. Gently but firmly squeeze the sides of each round so the flesh at the edges smooshes and cracks a bit. This will help the marrow penetrate the flesh of the potatoes. Arrange the rounds in a heavy enamelled baking dish (large enough to fit the potatoes and marrow bones in a single layer with a little space between them) and stand the marrow bones here and there between them. Drizzle the oil evenly over the potatoes and bones, sprinkle with the chillies and add a healthy sprinkle of Maldon salt over the top of each round and bone.

Pop the dish into the oven and cook, rotating the pan once or twice, until the undersides of the potatoes are deep brown, crispy and a bit sticky, 30 to 40 minutes. Flip the potatoes (if the oven is properly hot, they should release easily from the dish), but not the bones, and cook until the second sides are deep brown and crispy as well, 20 to 30 minutes more. Use a spatula to transfer the potatoes to a plate, spoon on a little of the fat from the baking dish, drizzle with the maple syrup and sprinkle with Maldon salt to taste.

serves 4 as a side

900g sweet potatoes, unpeeled, topped, tailed and cut crosswise into 4-cm thick rounds

3 tablespoons sea salt

450g centre-cut veal marrow bones, cut by your butcher into 4- to 5-cm lengths

55ml extra-virgin olive oil

4 dried pequín chillies, crumbled, or pinches of red pepper flakes

Maldon or another flaky sea salt

3 tablespoons pure maple syrup

# BROCCOLI WITH BACON

On its surface, there's not much to this dish, really. Yet, as with so much of the food I love, it's the small details in the cooking that result in something special. In this case, the pot is the key. If you use one that has nice high sides (anywhere from 15 to 25cm high) and that's wide enough to hold the broccoli snugly in one layer, the broccoli will fry in the porky fat but also steam a bit, so that by the time it's lightly browned it'll also be perfectly cooked – right at that sweet spot between crunchy and soft. Before I serve the dish, I like piling the onions and bacon on the broccoli so everyone can have a go at it with their fingers.

Heat the oil in a medium pot over high heat until it shimmers. Add the bacon and cook, stirring and scraping frequently, just until the edges of the bacon are browned and crispy, 2 to 3 minutes. Use a slotted spoon to transfer the bacon to a bowl, leaving the fat behind.

Add the broccoli to the bacon fat, stir it well, and top it with the onion. Cook, without stirring, until the broccoli begins to brown a bit, about 3 minutes, then stir and cook, stirring frequently, until the onion looks wilted and golden at the edges, about 3 minutes more.

Reduce the heat to medium-low and add the chillies and the reserved bacon. Cook, stirring occasionally, for about 5 minutes. Sprinkle on the salt and cook about 5 minutes more, until the broccoli stems are fully tender with a slight bite.

Transfer it all to a plate and squeeze on just enough lemon juice to provide brightness, not acidity. Serve straightaway.

serves 4 to 6 as a side

55ml extra-virgin olive oil

110g thinly sliced bacon, cut into 2-cm pieces

1 medium broccoli head, cut into 5-cm x 5-cm florets, stems trimmed, peeled and cut into 2.5-cm lengths

1 medium Spanish onion (about 225g), halved and thinly sliced

2 dried pequín chillies, crumbled, or pinches of red pepper flakes

1 teaspoon Maldon or another flaky sea salt

½ lemon

# BRAISED COLLARDS WITH BACON, VINEGAR AND CHILLIES

The first time I confronted collard greens – at Martha Lou's, a wonderful Charleston restaurant that specialises in soul food – I was a bit timid. I had never had collards in England. From what I'd heard, collards were strongly and unpleasantly flavoured – quite cabbagy and rough around the edges, at the opposite end of the spectrum from lemony, feminine chard. One bite of Martha Lou's collards, however, and I found that, like most notorious foods, when done right – as they were – they were delicious. Cooked with some smoky pork until they were very, very tender, these collards were right up my alley, especially since I come from England, the land of long-cooked vegetables.

My version begins with braised bacon. The braising liquid becomes a flavourful broth in which the collards cook, along with plenty of vinegar and chillies. Once the collards are ready, not only will they be supremely silky, though not as soft as the true Southern rendition, they will have absorbed the flavours of the pork and vinegar, which round off their rough edges.

Combine the bacon, garlic, onion and thyme in a large pot with 1.8 litres of water. Bring the water to a simmer over high heat. Cover, lower the heat to maintain a steady simmer and cook until the bacon is very tender (you should be able to insert a sharp knife by exerting only a little pressure) but not falling apart, about 1 hour. Uncover and discard the thyme stems.

Add the vinegar, tomatoes and chillies to the pot and stir. Increase the heat to high and bring the liquid to a boil. Let the liquid boil, stirring occasionally, until it has reduced by about half, about 25 minutes. It's fine if the bacon falls into large chunks, but try not to break it into stringy bits as you stir.

Meanwhile, cut the collards crosswise into 2.5-cm strips.

Add the sliced collards to the pot, pressing them down so they all fit.

serves 6 to 8 as a side

225g piece smoked slab bacon, halved

6 medium garlic cloves, halved lengthwise

1 small red onion (about 100g), peeled and halved

2 healthy thyme sprigs

110ml apple cider vinegar

70g drained, trimmed and coarsely chopped tinned whole tomatoes (see page 16)

2 to 4 dried ají dulce peppers or 4 to 6 dried pequín chillies, crumbled, or pinches of red pepper flakes

3 large bunches collard greens, stems thicker than 0.5cm removed

Maldon or another flaky sea salt

*a little beast goes a long way* **169**

Cover the pot, wait until the collards wilt slightly, 2 minutes or so, then stir well. Cover the pot again, lower the heat to maintain a steady simmer and cook, using tongs to toss and stir occasionally, until the collard leaves are very tender and the stems have just a slight bite, about 30 minutes.

Uncover, increase the heat a bit and cook at a strong simmer, stirring now and then, so some of the liquid cooks off, about 10 minutes. Have a taste. You might need to add some salt if your bacon wasn't salty to start with. Serve straightaway.

# STEAMED AUBERGINE WITH GROUND PORK AND THAI BASIL

This dish is definitely a Brummie girl's take on the classic Sichuan-style aubergine – if you are looking for 'authenticity,' fair warning. When I cook at home, I adapt dishes to fit my fussy ways. I latch on to the parts I like – Asian cooks often use meat almost like a seasoning, which I think is just grand – and put aside the ones I don't. Very rarely, for example, do I add sugar to savoury things. I happily eat Thai salads, Chinese stir-fries and other dishes that rely on a tablespoon or two for balance or contrast. But in my kitchen, I'd rather pull natural sweetness from garlic, onions, and the like. I like the result a lot, even though some might moan that it's not the real thing. It's a good job, then, that I don't run a Chinese restaurant. Serve this with steamy white rice and you've got a meal for four.

serves 4 to 6 as a side

2 medium aubergines (about 750g), topped, tailed, quartered lengthwise and cut crosswise into irregular 3-cm thick pieces

Maldon or another flaky sea salt

1 tablespoon neutral oil, such as safflower or grapeseed

55g finely chopped red onion (from about 1 small)

3 medium garlic cloves, finely chopped

225g ground pork

225ml Simple Chicken Stock (page 245)

1 tablespoon plus 1 teaspoon fish sauce

1 tablespoon soy sauce

A five-finger pinch of Thai basil (tender stems and leaves), roughly chopped

1 tablespoon lime juice

Put a steamer insert (or a colander, so long as the pot's lid can still close) in a large pot. Add enough water to reach about 1cm in depth, cover the pot and bring to a boil over high heat. Season the aubergine lightly with salt, add to the steamer, cover and steam until the pieces are fully tender and creamy, 12 to 15 minutes.

Meanwhile, heat the oil in a medium pot over high heat until it begins to smoke. Add the onion and garlic and cook, stirring constantly, until they begin to brown and smell sweet, about 2 minutes. Add the pork and cook, stirring, scraping the pot and breaking up the meat until it's golden brown in spots and just cooked through, 2 to 3 minutes. Add the stock, fish sauce and soy sauce, and let the liquid come to a simmer. Lower the heat to maintain a gentle simmer and cook, occasionally stirring and scraping the bottom of the pot, for about 5 minutes more, so the flavours come together.

Add the aubergine and basil to the pot and stir very gently. Raise the heat to medium-high. Cook, uncovered, at a vigorous simmer, for a few minutes, then add the lime juice and continue cooking, occasionally shaking the pan but not stirring, until the liquid has reduced to a slightly viscous consistency, 12 to 15 minutes. Serve while it's still steamy.

*a little beast goes a long way* **171**

# CABBAGE-STUFFED CABBAGE

Inexpensive and plentiful, lowly cabbage is rarely the star of a dish. Even when the vegetable headlines, as in stuffed cabbage, it typically takes a backseat to the meaty filling. Not so here, since I stuff cabbage with, well, more cabbage. I quite like the way the dish showcases two different textures of the same vegetable – the sturdiness of the boiled leaves and the silkiness of the braised cabbage inside them. Like most versions of stuffed cabbage, this one's hearty thanks to the meatiness of the vegetable, but it remains light and bright thanks to a finishing dose of lemon and Parmesan.

Combine the oil and butter in a wide heavy pot and set it over medium heat. When the butter melts, add the bacon and carrots first and then the onion on top. Sprinkle on 1½ teaspoons of the Maldon salt and pop on the lid. Cook, without stirring, until the bacon looks a bit translucent, 5 to 7 minutes. Have a stir and keep cooking, covered, stirring now and again and lowering the heat if necessary, until the onions are very soft but not coloured, about 15 minutes.

Meanwhile, remove and discard the outermost leaves of the cabbage. Carefully remove 12 large leaves and set aside. Halve, core and thinly slice the remaining cabbage until you get 750g. Reserve any remaining cabbage for another use.

Add the stock to the pot and bring it to a boil over high heat. Add the sliced cabbage and 1 teaspoon of the Maldon salt. Cover the pot, reduce the heat to medium and cook at a simmer, stirring now and then, until the cabbage is fully tender but not mushy, about 7 minutes. Take the pot off the heat.

Bring a medium pot of water to a boil over high heat and season it with sea salt until it tastes nice and salty. Boil the 12 reserved cabbage leaves in two batches until they're soft enough that you can fold them without breaking them, 3 to 4 minutes per batch. Drain them well, let them cool a bit and pat them dry.

serves 4 as a main

55ml extra-virgin olive oil, plus a healthy drizzle for finishing

50g unsalted butter, plus more for the baking dish

150g smoked bacon (slab or thick slices), cut into 0.5-cm cubes

110g carrots, peeled, topped, tailed and cut into 0.5-cm cubes

1 medium-large Spanish onion (about 330g), halved lengthwise and thinly sliced

2½ teaspoons plus a generous sprinkle Maldon or another flaky sea salt

2 Savoy cabbage heads (about 675g each)

225ml Simple Chicken Stock (page 245)

Sea salt

25g Parmesan cheese, finely grated

Freshly ground black pepper

½ lemon

Generously butter a large, heavy enamelled baking dish (large enough to hold the cabbage rolls snugly in a single layer). Lay the boiled leaves on a work surface, concave sides up. (If they have very thick stems, flip the leaves over and use a knife to shave off a bit of stem, then flip them back over.) Give the cabbage-bacon mixture a good stir, then use a slotted spoon to divide it evenly among the leaves, leaving a 1-cm border. Reserve the liquid for basting. Sprinkle a generous pinch of Parmesan onto each dollop of filling. Roll each leaf over the filling to form a fairly snug cylinder with open ends, then transfer it seam-side down to the baking dish.

Turn on the grill. Pop the baking dish in the oven about 10cm from the heat source and cook, basting occasionally with some of the reserved cooking liquid, until the cabbage rolls are very lightly browned on top and hot through, 3 to 5 minutes. Sprinkle the remaining Parmesan over the top, then add a generous sprinkle of Maldon salt, a few turns of black pepper and a drizzle of olive oil. Squeeze on just enough lemon so it all tastes bright, but not acidic. Eat straightaway.

# ROASTED MUSHROOMS WITH PANCETTA, PINE NUT BREADCRUMBS AND GOAT'S CHEESE

The porky sweetness of pancetta, the crunch of breadcrumbs and the tang of goat's cheese make this collection of roasted mushrooms moreish – each bite is a bit different and tempts you to take yet another. Taking a minute to carefully arrange the ingredients on a baking sheet just before they go into the oven also makes the dish special. I like to position the mushrooms just so, so the larger ones get good and tender and the smaller ones get a bit crispy. I tuck the thyme between the mushrooms so it doesn't burn. I wrap the pancetta in and around the mushrooms, because, well, it just feels right. My favourite part comes at the end when everything is all roasty and the juices have pooled in the pan. I tip the juices into a small pot, reduce them so their flavour concentrates, then spoon them back on.

Position a rack in the centre of the oven and preheat to 200°C/gas 6. Line a large baking sheet with baking parchment.

Halve the portobello caps (I like to cut on a diagonal instead of vertically here) and arrange the halves gill-side down on the baking sheet so the cut sides face each other and the corner of one of the halves is propped up on the corner of the other. Leave about 2.5cm of space between each pair. Divide the oyster mushrooms more or less evenly among the portobello pairs, arranging them here and there around and on top of the portobellos. Lay two pancetta slices on each pair. I like to curl them around the oyster mushrooms and tuck an end under the portobellos. Tuck 2 of the thyme sprigs between each pair of portobello halves. Arrange any larger maitake clusters around the portobellos and put small ones on top.

Divide the garlic slices and the butter (one piece per portobello pair) in little blobs here and there on top of the mushrooms. Over each

serves 6 as a side

6 medium portobello mushrooms, stems removed, caps peeled

225g oyster mushrooms, thick stems trimmed, mushrooms separated

12 thin, long slices pancetta

12 thyme sprigs

225g maitake mushrooms, thick stems trimmed, separated into smaller clusters

3 medium garlic cloves, very thinly sliced

50g unsalted butter, cut into 6 more or less even pieces

1¾ teaspoons Maldon or another flaky sea salt

6 tablespoons extra-virgin olive oil, plus a healthy drizzle for finishing

75g slightly stale rustic bread, such as filone, crust discarded, pulled into about 2.5-cm pieces

(continued on next page)

*a little beast goes a long way* **175**

portion, sprinkle about ¼ teaspoon of the Maldon salt, drizzle about 1½ teaspoons of the olive oil, and pour 2 tablespoons of water.

Roast in the oven until the portobellos are fully tender (a sharp knife inserted in the thickest part should meet very little resistance), the maitake mushrooms have browned a bit and the pancetta is slightly brown at the edges but still a bit floppy, 30 to 40 minutes. After 15 minutes and occasionally thereafter, take the tray from the oven, tip it so the juices pool and use a spoon to baste each portion. (If there is barely any juice, pour 55ml or so of water onto the tray.)

Meanwhile, put the bread in a food processor and pulse to form very coarse crumbs (a mixture of pebbly bits and chunks, 1cm at the largest). Put the crumbs in a medium cast-iron frying pan along with the pine nuts, toss well, and add the remaining 3 tablespoons of olive oil. Set the pan over high heat, wait for the oil to sizzle, and cook, tossing and stirring constantly, until the bread is crunchy and the pine nuts are peanut-butter brown, about 3 minutes. Drain the crumbs and pine nuts in a sieve, give them a good shake and transfer to kitchen paper to fully drain. Sprinkle on a little salt.

When the mushrooms are ready, carefully tip the pan and let the liquid run off into a small saucepan. Bring it to a boil over high heat and cook until it reduces a bit and tastes flavourful and a bit salty, about 5 minutes.

Use a spatula to transfer each portion to plates. Sprinkle on more salt to taste, drizzle on a little olive oil, then add a squeeze of lemon for brightness, not acidity, and a spoonful or two of the reduced mushroom liquid. Sprinkle on the breadcrumb mixture, put large pieces of the cheese here and there, and add the rocket. Dig in straightaway.

40g pine nuts

½ lemon

About 75g young goat's cheese

A handful of delicate, peppery rocket

chilly weather treats

# WINTER-SQUASH PANCAKES WITH SQUASH SYRUP AND PECAN BUTTER

Winter squash is a perfect breakfast component, as breakfast is much the same as squash: both can go in either a savoury or sweet direction. Some mornings I crave smooshed roasted squash on toast with floppy bacon and fried eggs. On others I look to this dish, in which the squash provides earthy sweetness to the batter and the maple syrup as well. I have a bit of fun serving the pancakes in a big old stack, tucking a couple slivers of pecan butter between each cake, topping the stack with a good knob of it, too, then pouring on the syrup at the table so it dribbles dramatically down the sides.

Preheat the oven to 200°C/gas 6. Put the squash in a heavy enamelled baking dish large enough to fit the squash in more or less one layer. Pour in 55ml of water, cover the dish tightly with foil and bake, stirring once, until the squash is very soft but not falling apart, about 45 minutes. If there's still water in the dish, remove the foil and bake just until the water's gone, about 5 minutes more. Let the squash cool a bit and purée it in a food processor until very smooth.

Lower the oven heat to 100°C/gas ¼ .

Combine the flour, polenta, bicarbonate of soda, baking powder, sugar and salt in a large mixing bowl and whisk well. Add the buttermilk, milk, egg and 350g of the squash purée and whisk until the mixture is smooth.

Stir together the maple syrup and 230g of the remaining squash purée in a small pot, reserving the remaining squash for another purpose. Gently heat the mixture until it's warm and keep it warm over very low heat.

Preheat a heavy griddle over medium heat until it's good and hot, then reduce the heat to medium-low. Use kitchen paper to rub a thin

makes sixteen
10- to 12-cm pancakes

450g peeled, seeded and cubed (about 4cm) butternut squash

125g plain flour

120g stone-ground polenta

1½ teaspoons bicarbonate of soda

1½ teaspoons baking powder

1 tablespoon plus 2 teaspoons granulated sugar

¼ teaspoon sea salt

225ml well-shaken buttermilk

220ml whole milk

1 large egg

165ml pure maple syrup

A few glugs of extra-virgin olive oil

About 6 tablespoons room-temperaure Spiced Pecan Butter (page 183) or plain salted butter layer of oil onto the griddle. Cook the pancakes in batches (use about 3 tablespoons batter per pancake), flipping them once with a sturdy spatula, until they're golden brown on both sides and fully cooked, 6 to 8 minutes. Transfer the pancakes to a plate and keep them in the warm oven. Between each batch, rub a little more oil on the griddle.

Serve in stacks with a pat of pecan butter tucked between each pancake and a couple on top, drizzle on the syrup and serve straightaway.

# SPICED PECAN BUTTER

makes about 225g

30g pecan halves

1 medium guajillo chilli (about 12 x 2.5cm), slit open, seeded and de-veined

½ teaspoon crumbled dried pequín chillies, or red pepper flakes

225g unsalted butter, at room temperature

2 tablespoons pure maple syrup

½ teaspoon sea salt

Position a rack in the centre of the oven and preheat to 180°C/gas 4. Spread the pecans in a single layer on a small baking sheet and bake, tossing occasionally, until they're aromatic but not coloured, 3 to 5 minutes. Transfer them to a cutting board, let them cool, and roughly chop until no bits are larger than 0.5cm.

Preheat a cast-iron frying pan over medium heat, add the guajillo, and toast, flipping once and occasionally pressing down on the chilli, until aromatic, 1 to 2 minutes. Let it cool, combine in a spice grinder with the pequín chillies, and buzz to a fine powder.

Combine the pecans, chilli powder (or red pepper flakes), butter, maple syrup and salt in a bowl and mix and mash until the ingredients are very well distributed. Spread the butter in a rough log shape on a piece of clingfilm, roll the wrap tightly around the butter and twist the edges to seal.

Use it straightaway, refrigerate for up to 5 days, or cut into portions and freeze in airtight packages for up to 1 month.

# ROASTED TREVISO WITH BREADCRUMBS AND GORGONZOLA

Treviso, a type of radicchio with longer leaves, is one of my pet vegetables. I love how the burgundy leaves contrast with the pure white stems. I love how astringent Treviso is, how after you handle it, its bitterness stays on your fingertips. But not everyone enjoys this quality and for those people, this dish is the answer. As the Treviso roasts, its bitterness mellows, the hearts get creamy, and the leaves go slightly crispy at the edges. And the sweetness of the pine-nut breadcrumbs, the acidity of the vinaigrette and the saltiness of the cheese all balance the whisper of bitterness remaining.

Position a rack in the centre of the oven and preheat to 200°C/gas 6.

Put the pine nuts in a mortar and pound until they're crushed to the texture of couscous. Pop them in a bowl. Combine the garlic and 1 teaspoon of the salt in the mortar and pound to a coarse paste, then add the marjoram and pound to a fine paste. Add the pine nuts, breadcrumbs, 55ml of the olive oil and 1 tablespoon of water to the mortar and stir well.

Slice into the root ends of the Treviso, about 4cm into the head. You're not trying to split the halves; this is just to help the heat penetrate this particularly dense part. Arrange the halves cut-sides up in a heavy enamelled baking dish just big enough to fit them in a single layer.

Working with one Treviso half at a time and separating the leaves carefully with your hands so they stay attached, use a spoon to tuck and spread a heaping tablespoon or so of the breadcrumb mixture onto the bottom leaf, another between the leaves near the middle, and another between the leaves near but not quite at the top of the halves. Sprinkle the remaining breadcrumb mixture on the top of each Treviso half.

Drizzle the root ends with a little olive oil and sprinkle with salt.

40g pine nuts

1 medium garlic clove, peeled

1¼ teaspoons plus a generous pinch Maldon or another flaky sea salt

A five-finger pinch of marjoram leaves

55g slightly coarse dried breadcrumbs

55ml plus 3 tablespoons extra-virgin olive oil, plus more for drizzling

3 medium heads Treviso (about 450g), root ends trimmed of brown bits but left intact, outermost leaves removed, halved lengthwise

2 teaspoons red wine vinegar

175g Gorgonzola, cut into 12 rustic-looking chunks

75g rocket

Cover the dish tightly with foil and bake until the root ends are fully soft and creamy, about 35 minutes. Remove the foil, increase the temperature to its highest setting and keep roasting, rotating the pan once, until the Treviso leaves are shrivelled and a bit crispy, and the visible breadcrumbs are golden brown, 10 to 15 minutes more.

Meanwhile, in a small bowl, whisk together the vinegar, the remaining 3 tablespoons of the oil and ¼ teaspoon of the Maldon salt until the mixture looks creamy. Drizzle half of the vinaigrette over the heads while they're still hot.

Let the Treviso cool to warm or room temperature. Divide the Treviso among 6 plates. Put 2 chunks of Gorgonzola next to each head. Right before you're ready to serve, gently toss the rocket with the remaining dressing in a bowl and pile some next to each head.

# DOSA WITH CURRIED CAULIFLOWER AND YOGURT

I don't think I'd ever had a dosa, a type of crêpe made from a fermented lentil and rice batter, before coming to New York. My hometown of Birmingham has a big Pakistani and Indian population, but not so many people from South India, where the dosa comes from. Vegetarianism goes hand in hand with religion there, so creative cooks have come up with an entire universe of incredibly tasty, sophisticated and satisfying meatless food. Even though the dosa comes from a place with a hot climate, I find it perfect for eating in chilly weather.

The first time I had a dosa, I ordered a couple of types at a restaurant, not quite knowing what to expect. The waiter arrived bearing this massive golden, crispy cylinder, which was almost twice as long as the plate it came on. Another version was smaller, softer and spongier, but just as delicious. Its fermented tang reminded me of Parmesan cheese. I ate quickly, because they were so good and because I could barely wait to have a go at making them myself. It turns out that once you get the hang of it, they're pretty easy to replicate at home (well, not so much those massive ones). Of course, if you're like me, you'll be shit-scared at mucking up the first few. To help, this recipe makes plenty of batter. And even your unsuccessful practice dosa will be tasty to nibble on.

### make the dosa batter

Combine the rice and the two types of dal in a large mixing bowl and add 2.2 litres of water. Stir well and cover the bowl with cheesecloth or a lid left slightly ajar. Leave the bowl at room temperature (and away from any cool draughts) to ferment until the mixture smells slightly sour and looks a bit frothy, about 24 hours. If you like your dosa a little more sour, which I do, let it ferment for another 12 to 24 hours.

Drain the rice mixture, reserving 900ml of the liquid. Blend the rice

serves 4 to 6 as a main

FOR THE DOSA BATTER

400g basmati rice

200g white urad dal (see note, page 189)

50g chana dal (see note, page 189)

1 teaspoon Maldon salt

FOR COOKING AND FILLING THE DOSAS

Several teaspoons extra-virgin olive oil

Maldon or another flaky sea salt

Curried Cauliflower with Peas (page 190), warm

Generous 75g Greek yogurt

A small handful of delicate coriander sprigs, roughly chopped mixture with 675ml of the reserved liquid until completely smooth, gradually adding up to another 225ml of the liquid if necessary to achieve a texture like that of double cream. When you're ready to make the dosa, stir in the salt until it has dissolved.

## cook and fill the dosa

Heat a large nonstick frying pan over medium heat until it's good and hot. Before you cook the first dosa, add about ½ teaspoon of oil to the pan and swirl the pan to coat the bottom as best you can. Between dosa, wipe the pan clean.

Stir the batter well before making each dosa. Spoon about 3 tablespoons of the batter into the centre of the pan and using an implement with a flat bottom, such as a metal measuring cup, spread the batter into a very thin round about 20cm in diameter. Start in the centre and spread the batter outwards using a circular motion. You need a really light touch to get the batter nice and thin without creating any big holes (tiny holes form naturally and that's a good thing). You'll get better with each one you make – and you have plenty of batter, so don't fret if you bungle the first few. I often do.

After spreading the batter, add a very light drizzle of oil and a light sprinkle of salt to the surface of the dosa. Let the dosa cook, without messing with it, until the edges begin to brown and lift from the pan and the underside is a light golden colour, 1½ to 2 minutes. Use a spatula to gently lift an edge, then transfer the dosa to a plate – it should come away from the pan easily and cleanly. Spoon 130 to 200g of the curried cauliflower to one side of the dosa. Add a dollop of yogurt and a generous pinch of the chopped coriander. Fold the dosa over the filling to make a semicircle and serve straightaway while you get to work on the remaining dosa.

*Note: Urad dal are small black beans that resemble split lentils, and come in several forms: whole, split, and split and husked. For this recipe, buy the latter form, which is off-white in colour. Chana dal is a small sibling of the chickpea that has been split and husked. Both are available at Indian markets and online.*

# CURRIED CAULIFLOWER with PEAS

Although I originally designed this as filling for my take on the South Indian crêpe called dosa (page 187), I'd eat it on its own any day with some basmati rice to make it a meal. I'm by no means an expert on Indian cooking. I just love it. I fell for the food growing up in Birmingham, where good curry shops sometimes seem to outnumber good pubs. I idolise Madhur Jaffrey, who did for Indian cooking in America what Marcella Hazan did for Italian cooking. Who knows, she might taste this and take a dim view. But I think it's quite tasty.

Heat the oil in a medium pot over medium-high heat until it smokes lightly. Add the onion, stir well, and cook, stirring occasionally, until wilted and just beginning to colour, about 3 minutes. Add the garlic and chilli and cook, stirring, until the onion has browned in spots, 3 to 5 minutes more.

Add the cauliflower and coriander stems to the pot and cook, stirring occasionally, just until the cauliflower has picked up some of the brown colour from the onion, about 2 minutes. Add the tomatoes, garam masala and salt, and cook, stirring frequently, until the tomato is thick and jammy, about 5 minutes.

Stir in the peas and 110ml of water, scraping the sides and bottom of the pot to get at that nice browned stuff. Pop a lid on the pot, reduce the heat to maintain a steady simmer, and cook, stirring occasionally, until the cauliflower is fully tender but not mushy and the liquid has thickened a bit, about 20 minutes. (You might have to remove the lid for the last 5 minutes to help the liquid evaporate.) Stir in the yogurt, turn off the heat and let the curry sit covered for a few minutes so the flavours can meld. Serve straightaway.

The curry keeps for a day or two in the fridge. Add a splash of water and gently warm it before serving.

serves 4 as a side

3 tablespoons extra-virgin olive oil

1 medium red onion (about 225g), halved lengthwise and thinly sliced

3 medium garlic cloves, thinly sliced

1 red Thai or another small, very spicy fresh chilli, thinly sliced (including seeds)

1 small head cauliflower, trimmed and cut into 5-cm x 5-cm florets

2 generous tablespoons very thinly sliced coriander stems

150g drained, trimmed and finely chopped tinned whole tomatoes (see page 16)

1 tablespoon garam masala (preferably homemade, page 240)

1 tablespoon Maldon or another flaky sea salt

300g frozen baby peas

1 heaped tablespoon Greek yogurt

# CURRIED PARSNIP SOUP

I remember making my first curries and fretting that they were quite bland. Now I know it was because I was being French with the shallots, rather than taking them quite dark, as an Indian cook would, to add rich complexity. The coconut milk and garam masala are, of course, key players in this soup, but the unsung heroes of the dish are actually the apples. Their acidity is a perfect counterpoint to the sweetness of the parsnips, and it lends a hint of brightness to the deep flavour of the shallots.

Heat the oil in a medium pot over medium-high heat until it smokes lightly. Add the shallots, stir well and cook, stirring and scraping the pan frequently so nothing burns, until they're very soft, sweet and deep golden brown, about 10 minutes. Add the garlic and cook, stirring frequently, until it's light golden brown, 2 to 3 minutes.

Add the parsnips, apples, garam masala, salt and 1.1 litres of water and stir well. Turn the heat to high, bring the water to a boil, then lower the heat to maintain a gentle simmer. Cook for 20 minutes or so, then add the coconut milk and cream. Bring the liquid back to a gentle simmer and cook until the parsnips and apples are fully soft, about 45 minutes more.

Pour the soup into a large mixing bowl. Working in batches, blend the soup (be careful when blending hot liquids) until very smooth and silky, adding each batch back to the pot. Season to taste with salt and serve it straightaway or keep it in the fridge for up to 3 days.

serves 6 to 8

55ml plus 2 tablespoons extra-virgin olive oil

225g shallots (about 3 large), halved lengthwise and thinly sliced

4 medium garlic cloves, very thinly sliced

1kg parsnips, peeled, topped, tailed and cut into 2.5-cm pieces

500g sweet-tart apples, such as Empire (about 3), peeled and cut into 2.5-cm pieces

2 teaspoons garam masala (preferably homemade, page 240)

1 tablespoon plus 1 teaspoon Maldon or another flaky sea salt

225ml well-stirred tinned coconut milk

120ml double cream

# SLOW-ROASTED LEEKS WITH WALNUT BREADCRUMBS

Leeks are wonderful when prepared in the French bistro style: simply poached, then bathed in vinaigrette. I tweak the classic, slow-roasting the poached leeks to accentuate their sweetness and succulence, and adding contrast with walnut breadcrumbs that get crunchy as the leeks get softer. While leeks vinaigrette is typically served cold or at room temperature, I like to dress the leeks straight from the oven and eat the dish while it's good and hot. For this dish, choose leeks that have a good long portion (about 23cm) of white and light green.

Position a rack in the centre of the oven and preheat to 200°C/gas 6.

Cut off the dark green parts from the leeks. Remove and discard the outermost layer (you might have to remove the second layer as well if it feels woody). Trim the roots and any brown bits but keep the root end intact. Cut each leek crosswise to separate the white part from the light green part. Make a lengthwise cut through half of each piece, leaving the rest of the half intact (this will help with swishing out the grit). Soak the leeks in a big bowl of cold water for a few minutes, gently separating the layers with your fingers to expose any gritty bits and swishing a bit, then drain them.

Meanwhile, combine the halved garlic head, lemon zest, thyme, bay leaves, 2 teaspoons of the salt and 1.3 litres of water in a large, wide pot. Bring to a boil over high heat and boil for 5 minutes or so, just to infuse the liquid with flavour.

Add the white leek halves to the water, wait a minute, then add the light green halves. Let the water come back to a boil, then lower the heat to maintain a steady simmer. Cook, carefully turning the leeks occasionally, until they're just tender (a sharp knife inserted in a leek should meet with a little resistance), 8 to 12 minutes. Using a spider or slotted spoon, carefully transfer the leeks to kitchen paper to drain

serves 4 to 6 as a side

5 large leeks (about 1.3kg), each about 4cm wide

1 large head garlic, halved crosswise, plus 1 medium clove, roughly chopped

4 strips (8 x 2cm) lemon zest

4 small thyme sprigs

2 fresh bay leaves

2½ teaspoons Maldon or another flaky sea salt

55g walnut halves

A five-finger pinch of delicate flat-leaf parsley sprigs, roughly chopped

30g coarse dried breadcrumbs

110ml extra-virgin olive oil

2 tablespoons roasted walnut oil

1 tablespoon plus 1 teaspoon red wine vinegar

2 teaspoons Dijon mustard

and let them sit until cool to the touch. Pat them dry. Reserve a generous tablespoon of the cooking liquid.

Combine the garlic clove and remaining ½ teaspoon salt in a mortar and pound to a fine paste. Add the walnuts and gently pound them so they break into 0.5 to 1-cm pieces. Scoop out a good tablespoon or two of the walnuts and set aside. Add the parsley to the garlic-walnut mixture in the mortar and pound to a coarse paste. Stir in the reserved walnuts, the breadcrumbs, and 55ml of the olive oil.

Heat the remaining 55ml of olive oil in a heavy enamelled baking dish (large enough to hold the leeks side by side with a little room to spare) over medium-high heat until it shimmers. Add the leeks and cook, carefully flipping them over once, until they're lightly browned on both sides, about 3 minutes. Line them up prettily in the dish so they're touching, then scatter the breadcrumb mixture on top.

Pop the dish in the oven and bake, rotating the pan once, until the crumbs are crispy, the nuts are toasty and the leeks are fully tender, 20 to 30 minutes.

Meanwhile, whisk together the walnut oil, vinegar, mustard and the reserved leek cooking liquid until the mixture looks creamy. Drizzle it over the hot leeks and serve straightaway.

# BUTTERY, NOT-QUITE-MUSHY BRUSSELS SPROUTS

Like most Brits, my fondness for sprouts goes way back. I like them every which way. When they're roasted and crispy. When they're cooked to a soft crunch in a pan with some fatty pork product. When they're boiled and lavishly buttered. When I was a girl, I even adored the sprouts a certain loving relative made in the pressure cooker, which turned grey and went so squishy that they collapsed in my mouth. I might not care to eat those today, but they certainly gave me an appreciation for sprouts cooked well past crunchy. Like these sprouts, which take a quick trip in boiling water before cooking slowly in quite a bit of butter. By the time they're done, they've absorbed that dairy flavour, the outer leaves have gone a little chewy and sticky, and the insides become soft – but not quite mushy.

serves 4 to 6 as a side

Sea salt

900g large Brussels sprouts, bottoms trimmed and blemished outer leaves discarded

200g unsalted butter, cut into a few pieces

1 teaspoon Maldon or another flaky sea salt

Bring a medium pot of water to a boil and add enough sea salt so it tastes a bit less salty than the sea. Add the sprouts and cook until they're still quite firm, but you can smoothly insert a knife into one while applying pressure, 6 to 7 minutes. Drain the sprouts well.

Melt the butter in a large cast-iron frying pan (wide enough for the Brussels sprouts to fit in a single layer) over medium-high heat, adjusting the heat so it bubbles away but doesn't brown. Add the sprouts to the butter, reduce the heat if necessary to cook at a rapid bubble, gently turning them over as they colour, until they're very soft (but not mushy) and deep brown on the outsides, about 15 minutes – a bit more if you like them mushy.

Stir in the Maldon salt and use a slotted spoon to transfer the sprouts to a plate, leaving the remaining butter behind. Eat straightaway.

# ROASTED CARROTS
# WITH GARLIC CONFIT AND THYME

Just as a pork chop or veal breast might benefit from starting on the hob before being finished in the oven, so do carrots. Jumpstarting the browning on the stove helps bring out the carrots' sweetness. Then, once their flavour has concentrated in the oven and the carrots are fully and evenly tender – I'm not a fan of crunchy roasted carrots or those that are crispy outside and mushy inside – your job is done. The addition of butter, thyme, garlic and just enough lemon to perk up the palate is just the whipped cream on the pudding. When the carrots no longer scald your fingers, you can eat them with your hands, occasionally nabbing a garlic clove and squeezing the skin so the soft, sweet flesh pops into your mouth.

serves 4 to 6 as a side

16 medium garlic cloves, unpeeled

About 150ml extra-virgin olive oil

20 small carrots (the size of index fingers), scrubbed well but unpeeled and all but 1cm of the tops removed

1 teaspoon Maldon or another flaky sea salt

1 tablespoon unsalted butter

4 thyme sprigs

½ lemon

Put the garlic cloves in a small pot and add just enough olive oil to completely cover them. Set the pot over medium heat and wait until you hear a quiet sizzle. Reduce the heat to low. Continue to cook the cloves until they are smooshably soft, 30 to 45 minutes. Remove the cloves and measure out 2 tablespoons of the oil (the rest of the slightly garlicky oil will keep in an airtight container in the fridge for up to 1 month).

Position a rack in the centre of the oven and preheat to its highest setting. Add the 2 tablespoons of garlic oil to an ovenproof cast-iron frying pan just big enough to hold the carrots in one layer and set the pan over high heat. When the oil smokes lightly, add the carrots, sprinkle on the salt and use tongs to toss the carrots well. Cook, shaking and turning over the carrots occasionally, until they're browned in spots, 6 to 8 minutes.

Add the butter to the pan, let it melt, and toss the carrots well. Add the garlic cloves, skin and all, and pop the pan in the oven. After a few minutes, add the thyme to the pan. Toss, then continue to roast, tossing once more, until the carrots are evenly tender, 10 to 15 minutes, depending on the size of your carrots.

Gently squeeze on just enough lemon juice to add brightness, but not acidity. Let the carrots cool a bit and serve warm.

# SPICED CARROTS WITH YOGURT

They bring back memories, these carrots. I used to serve them at the first incarnation of the John Dory, which Ken Friedman and I opened in 2008 before closing, rethinking, and reopening in the Ace Hotel a couple of years later. All is well now, but the closing was a sad time and one that's still hard for me to think about. Perhaps that's why I haven't served these carrots at any of my restaurants since, even though I love them so. The magic is in the way they're cut and cooked: slow cooking pieces with especially sharp edges means that not only do the carrots get good and sweet, but that those pointed edges get soft and fall off, mingling with the spices and yogurt to create a sort of coating for each carrot chunk. I add a spot of orange blossom water, which gives a whisper of flavour and aroma that you sense at the very beginning of each bite and again at the very end.

Combine the coriander and cumin seeds in a small pan, set the pan over medium-low heat and cook, shaking and tossing frequently, until the spices are very fragrant and smoke lightly, about 5 minutes. Transfer them to a bowl or plate to cool slightly, then grind them to a coarse powder in a spice grinder or mortar. Add the cardamom seeds and grind or pound to a fine powder.

Starting at the tapered end of each carrot, cut a piece on the diagonal that's about 2.5cm long, roll the carrot a quarter turn, cut another piece at the same angle, and so on. Heat 3 tablespoons of the oil in a medium pot (wide enough to hold the carrots snugly in more or less one layer) over high heat until it smokes lightly. Add the garlic and cook, stirring frequently, until it goes golden brown at the edges, about 1 minute.

Add the carrots, chilli, ground spices and salt to the pot, and have a good old stir. Cover the pot, lower the heat to medium and cook, stirring and later scraping the bottom occasionally, until the spices begin to stick to the pot, about 15 minutes. Add 55ml plus 2 tablespoons of water, stir, and cover the pot again.

serves 4 to 6 as a side

2 teaspoons coriander seeds

1 teaspoon cumin seeds

About 12 green cardamom pods, whacked with the flat of a chef's knife, pods discarded, seeds reserved (heaped ¼ teaspoon seeds)

1.1kg medium carrots without greens (about 10), peeled, topped and tailed

4 tablespoons extra-virgin olive oil, plus a drizzle for finishing

3 large garlic cloves, thinly sliced

1 red Thai or another small, very spicy fresh chilli, thinly sliced (including seeds)

2 teaspoons Maldon or another flaky sea salt

3 tablespoons Greek yogurt

2 teaspoons orange blossom water

A small handful of delicate coriander sprigs, roughly chopped

A five-finger pinch of mint leaves, roughly chopped at the last minute

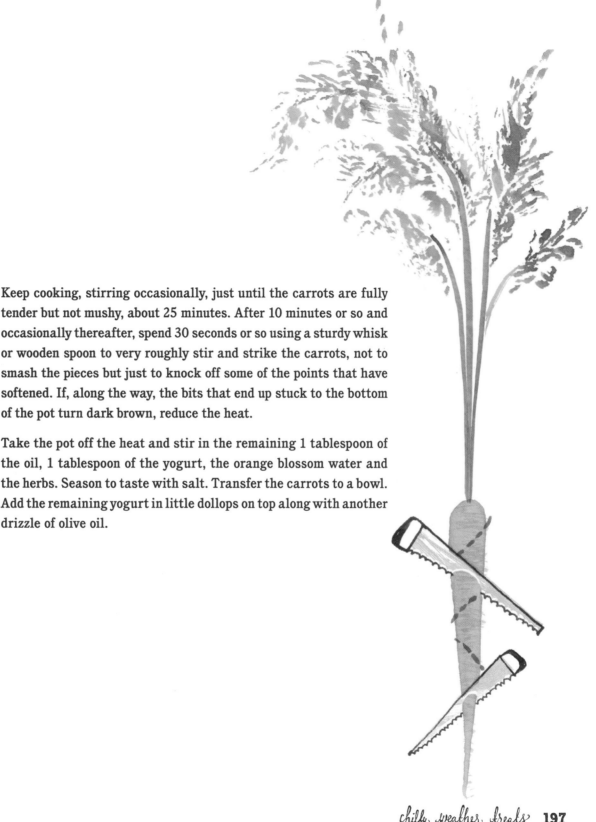

Keep cooking, stirring occasionally, just until the carrots are fully tender but not mushy, about 25 minutes. After 10 minutes or so and occasionally thereafter, spend 30 seconds or so using a sturdy whisk or wooden spoon to very roughly stir and strike the carrots, not to smash the pieces but just to knock off some of the points that have softened. If, along the way, the bits that end up stuck to the bottom of the pot turn dark brown, reduce the heat.

Take the pot off the heat and stir in the remaining 1 tablespoon of the oil, 1 tablespoon of the yogurt, the orange blossom water and the herbs. Season to taste with salt. Transfer the carrots to a bowl. Add the remaining yogurt in little dollops on top along with another drizzle of olive oil.

# VEGETABLE CRISPS WITH RED ZA'ATAR

At the end of a long winter, even my enthusiasm for root vegetables begins to flag a bit. And I'm an avowed root veg lover. That's when I turn to these colourful crisps, which make of the same old carrots and beetroot something special and fun. They're the most delicious things, these crisps. Every single one has its own character. Nibble a few at a time and you can still taste the earthy potato, the sweet beet. Not to mention they're very cute. Particularly the parsnips, which when sliced into rounds, fry up like little flowers.

While they're well worth the effort, crisps do require time and attention. Take care to slice the vegetables uniformly, applying even pressure as you work the mandoline. (In case you're afraid for your fingers, buy a few extra veg so you're not compelled to tempt fate.) The frying is quite simple, easier than many home cooks assume, though you'll want to make sure to tweak the heat if necessary and not overload the oil with veg, in order to maintain a consistent temperature. Once you master frying, you'll find yourself having a go with vegetables you didn't plan to fry. That's how I discovered fried beetroot leaves, which get a little lemony, almost like chard.

Using the mandoline, slice the parsnip, carrot and beetroot into uniformly thin (you're shooting for about 1.5-mm) pieces. Cut the parsnip into round slices and the carrot and beetroot into lengthwise slices. You might want to halve the carrots and beetroot lengthwise before slicing to make it easier to slice evenly. Five minutes or so before you're ready to fry, slice the potatoes lengthwise, put them in a bowl of water and gently toss with your hands to wash off some of the starch. Leave the potatoes in the bowl until you're ready to fry, but don't keep them in the water for more than 5 minutes or they will absorb too much water, making it difficult to fry them properly. Remove the thick centre vein from the reserved beetroot leaves and tear the leaves into large pieces. Keep each type of vegetable separate.

serves 4 to 8
as a snack

SPECIAL EQUIPMENT

A mandoline; an electric deep-fryer or a large, heavy pot, a deep-frying thermometer, a splatter screen; and a spider

1 medium parsnip (about 110g), peeled, topped and tailed

1 large carrot (about 225g), peeled, topped, tailed and halved crosswise

3 golf-ball-size beetroot, unpeeled, trimmed of roots and all but 2.5cm of stems, pert leaves reserved

225g waxy potatoes, unpeeled

Peanut, sunflower or vegetable oil for deep-frying

Sea salt

About 5 tablespoons Red Za'atar Spice (page 239)

Add the oil (the amount depends on your fryer's capacity) to your electric deep-fryer and heat to 180°C/350°F. Alternatively, clip a deep-frying thermometer to a heavy pot and add at least 8cm of oil. Heat the oil over high heat until it has reached 180°C/350°F. Line a large mixing bowl with kitchen paper for draining.

Drain the potatoes, pat them dry and fry them in batches (a good handful at a time), using a long spoon to keep them moving in the oil so they fry evenly and tweaking the heat as necessary to maintain the temperature as best you can. Fry until they're light golden brown and crispy, about 5 minutes. As each batch is done, use the fryer basket or a spider to transfer it to the kitchen-paper lined bowl. Immediately give the vegetables a gentle toss to help drain the oil, season with sea salt and transfer to a serving bowl.

Lower the heat to bring the oil temperature to a steady 170°C/325°F. One type at a time, fry the rest of the vegetables in batches the same way you fried the potatoes, until they're crispy. Fry the beetroot last, because it'll stain the oil. The frying will take about 3 minutes for the parsnips, about 5 minutes for the carrots, 1 minute for the beetroot leaves, and about 4 minutes for the beetroot. You'll want to add the cover to the electric fryer or use a splatter screen when you're frying the leaves, because they splatter.

The crisps will stay crispy for up to 1 hour. When you're ready to eat, sprinkle on the za'atar and serve straightaway.

vegetables

and cream

{a love affair}

# JANSSON'S TEMPTATION

No one can quite agree on who Jansson was. Yet I understand why he'd be tempted by this classic Swedish casserole of potatoes and cream. The traditional version includes pickled anchovy-like fish called sprats, but where I first encountered the dish – at Kensington Place – the chef, Rowley Leigh, used salted anchovies. I was smitten by the way they melded with the cream. I even like adding a few extra whole fillets to the baking dish right before popping it into the oven. As the whole thing bakes, the cream thickens, intensifying the umami quality of the anchovy. I add fennel to my version, which provides a meaty counterpoint to the velvety potatoes. The breadcrumbs on top add crunch and a sneaky pop of chilli. The whole thing is so rich you only need a little, but so good that you want quite a lot.

Bring a medium pot of water to a boil over high heat and season it with sea salt until it tastes a little less salty than the sea.

Cut the potatoes into approximately 8-cm x 2.5-cm wedges, then briefly rinse them under water and drain them. Add the potatoes to the boiling water, let the water return to a boil, and cook for about 4 minutes.

Meanwhile, halve the fennel bulbs lengthwise and cut each half through the root nub (so the wedges stay intact) into approximately 2.5-cm thick wedges. Cut the onion through the root nub into approximately 1-cm thick wedges.

When the 4 minutes have passed, add the fennel, let the water return to a boil, and cook just until both the potato and fennel are cooked through (you should be able to insert a sharp knife with only slight resistance), about 2 minutes or so. Transfer them to a colander and drain well.

Wipe the pot clean, add 55ml of the oil and the butter, and set the pot over medium-low heat. Once the butter melts, add the onion, halved

**serves 8 to 10 as a side**

Sea salt

900g large waxy potatoes (about 4), peeled

2 large fennel bulbs, stalks and outermost layer discarded, tender fronds reserved, root end trimmed of brown bits

1 large Spanish onion (about 450g), peeled, root end trimmed but left intact, halved through the root nub

55ml plus 2 tablespoons extra-virgin olive oil

2 tablespoons unsalted butter

13 medium garlic cloves, 12 halved lengthwise, 1 finely grated

7 salt-packed whole anchovies, soaked and filleted (see page 13)

4 strips (about 10 x 1cm) lemon zest

4 thyme sprigs

1 teaspoon fennel seeds, ground or pounded to a powder

950ml double cream

garlic, anchovies, lemon zest, thyme and ground fennel. Have a stir, cover the pot, and cook, stirring now and again, until the onions are very soft but not coloured, about 20 minutes.

Position a rack in the centre of the oven and preheat to 230°C/gas 8.

Add the cream and 1 tablespoon of the Maldon salt to the pot and raise the heat to medium-high. Bring the cream to a boil, scraping off any anchovy stuck to the sides of the pot. Lower the heat and simmer for 5 minutes. Add the potatoes and fennel and raise the heat to medium-high again. Bring the cream to a boil, then turn off the heat. Discard the lemon peel and thyme stems.

Use a slotted spoon to transfer the potato, fennel, and onion to a large, heavy enamelled baking dish so they're evenly distributed and in more or less one layer. Pour the cream mixture over the vegetables and give the dish a gentle shake to distribute it evenly. Bake, uncovered, until the cream has thickened slightly and browned in spots, about 25 minutes.

Meanwhile, roughly chop some of the reserved fennel fronds. Working in batches so as not to overload your food processor, add the bread and a five-finger pinch of the fennel fronds (saving the remaining fronds for garnish), then pulse until you have very coarse breadcrumbs (a mixture of pebbly bits and chunks, 1cm at the largest). Transfer the crumbs to a mixing bowl, add the remaining 2 tablespoons of oil, the grated garlic, a pinch of salt, the Parmesan and the chillies, then give it a good old mix with your hands.

Remove the dish from the oven and sprinkle the breadcrumbs evenly over the top. Turn on the grill and return the dish to the oven or under the grill. Grill, rotating the pan occasionally, until the breadcrumbs go golden brown and crispy, 5 to 10 minutes.

Let the casserole cool for a few minutes, then grab another five-finger pinch of the fronds and sprinkle it over the top. Have at it.

1 tablespoon plus a pinch of Maldon or another flaky sea salt

225g slightly stale rustic bread, such as filone, crust discarded, pulled into about 2.5-cm pieces

25g Parmesan cheese, finely grated

10 dried pequín chillies, crumbled, or pinches of red pepper flakes

# MORELS WITH MADEIRA CREAM ON TOAST

I wouldn't be much of an Englishwoman if I didn't fancy mushrooms on toast. This is a luxurious version, made with meaty, woodsy morels lavished with cream. Madeira lends its nutty complexity to the dish and cuts the richness with its acidity.

Morels can be spendy, so feel free to bulk up 100g with cremini or oyster mushrooms. If you're itching for morels but it's not quite spring, you can get away with using the high-quality dried version. To get the right amount for this recipe, soak 50g of dried morels in 450ml of warm water for half an hour, then squeeze them gently to rid them of excess water.

Melt the butter in a medium pot over high heat until it froths. Add the shallots and salt, stir, and reduce the heat to medium-low. Cook, stirring, just until the shallots have a kiss of brown, about 3 minutes. Stir in the morels and cook, stirring now and then, until the mushrooms are just cooked through, about 5 minutes.

Add the stock, cream, 75ml of the Madeira, and the tarragon. Raise the heat to high, bring to a boil and cook, stirring occasionally, just until the liquid has thickened slightly, about 3 minutes. Pour in the remaining 75ml of the Madeira and continue to boil until the liquid thickens just enough to coat the back of a spoon, about 2 minutes. Stir in the crème fraîche and take the pot off the heat.

Toast the bread just until the surface is crispy, then rub the cut sides of the garlic on the surface of each slice. Divide the toast among 4 plates, spoon on the mushrooms, and sprinkle on the remaining tarragon.

serves 4 as a side

3 tablespoons unsalted butter

1 large shallot, finely chopped (about 55g)

1 teaspoon Maldon or another flaky sea salt

Scant 225g fresh morel mushrooms, halved lengthwise if large and cleaned (see 'Cleaning Wild Mushrooms', page 135)

150ml Simple Chicken Stock (page 245)

160ml double cream

150ml dry Madeira (preferably special reserve)

A five-finger pinch of tarragon leaves, roughly chopped, plus more for finishing

1 tablespoon crème fraîche

4 thick slices crusty country bread

1 medium garlic clove, halved

# CREAMED SPINACH

If you've made it this far in the book, you can probably tell I'm partial to a bit of cream. But my version of creamed spinach is – surprisingly, perhaps – more about highlighting the earthy, lemony flavour and slightly meaty texture of this under-appreciated green. White wine and lemon zest keep the dish's richness from becoming heavy. And the anchovies provide sneaky complexity: no one will know they're there unless you tell.

serves 4 to 6 as a side

1kg hearty spinach (not baby), all but 2.5cm of stems trimmed

4 tablespoons extra-virgin olive oil

2 large shallots (a generous 100g), cut into thin rings

1½ teaspoons Maldon or another flaky sea salt

2 medium garlic cloves, thinly sliced

1 tablespoon thyme leaves, finely chopped

3 salt-packed whole anchovies, soaked and filleted (see page 13)

225ml white wine

360ml double cream

¼ teaspoon finely grated lemon zest

Several gratings of nutmeg

Several turns of freshly ground black pepper

In a large, wide pot, bring 110ml of water to a boil over high heat. Add the spinach (in batches if necessary) and pop on a lid. Cook until the spinach at the bottom wilts, about 2 minutes. Stir well and keep cooking with the lid on until all the spinach is fully wilted but not cooked to buggery, about 2 minutes more. Drain the spinach in a colander, pressing the spinach with a wooden spoon to squeeze out some of the water. Spread the spinach on a large plate so it doesn't carry on cooking and let it cool to the touch, then squeeze the spinach to remove as much water as you can.

Wipe out the pot. Pour in 3 tablespoons of the oil and heat it over medium heat until it shimmers. Add the shallots and ½ teaspoon of the salt and cook, stirring occasionally, until translucent, about 3 minutes. Stir in the garlic and cook until it's lightly golden at the edges, about 2 minutes. Stir in the thyme and cook until the shallots are soft and shrink a bit, about 3 minutes more. Push the shallot-garlic mixture to the side, add the anchovies to the oil on the empty side, and cook without stirring until they're lightly browned, about 2 minutes. Stir the anchovies and vegetables together.

Pour in the white wine, increase the heat to high, and bring it to a boil. Boil until the wine has reduced so that it just barely covers the bottom of the pan, 3 to 5 minutes. Pour in the cream, let it come to a boil, and cook, stirring occasionally, until the mixture thickens enough to coat the back of a metal spoon, 5 to 7 minutes. Sprinkle in the spinach, unfurling the clumps as you add it to the pot, and cook, stirring often, until it's hot through, about 3 minutes.

Stir in the lemon zest, nutmeg and pepper along with the remaining 1 tablespoon of oil and 1 teaspoon of salt. Cook, stirring, just until the spinach is fully tender but retains its integrity and the flavours come together, about 3 minutes. Eat straightaway.

# SWEET-CORN ICE CREAM WITH BUTTERSCOTCH

When I was first served corn ice cream, I thought the guy who made it was having a laugh. To me, corn meant succotash, soup and steamy ears buttered and sprinkled with crunchy sea salt. It did not mean dessert. Yet while it took me a good minute to get my head around the idea, it took me only about five seconds to eat every last bit. Of course, corn ice cream makes perfect sense – corn is good mates with dairy, and during summer the veg is sweeter than strawberries, peaches and other fruits commonly spotted in ice cream. A healthy drizzle of butterscotch and a scattering of caramel popcorn add sweet-salty complexity and crunch.

## make the butterscotch

Combine the cream, whisky and salt in a measuring cup with a spout. Use a knife to scrape the seeds of the vanilla bean into the cup and stir well.

Combine the granulated sugar, butter, brown sugar, corn syrup and 55ml of water in a medium saucepan with high sides. Set it over high heat and bring to a boil. Attach a candy thermometer to the pan and boil until the mixture reaches 120°C/245°F. Remove the pan from the heat and gradually whisk in the cream mixture. Let the mixture cool to room temperature. You'll have about 180ml of butterscotch.

Use straightaway or stir once more and keep in an airtight container in the fridge for up to 2 weeks. Gently reheat until warm before using.

## make the ice cream

Cut the corn kernels from the cobs, reserving the cobs. Cut the cobs crosswise into a few pieces. Combine the kernels and cobs in a medium pot along with the cream, milk, salt and 55g of the sugar. Bring the liquid to a simmer, stirring occasionally, over medium-high heat, then turn off the heat, cover the pot and let the mixture steep at room temperature for at least 2 hours or in the fridge for as long as 12 hours. Remove the cobs, gently scraping them with a spoon to get at any

**makes about 1½ pints plus 180ml of butterscotch**

SPECIAL EQUIPMENT

A 1.8 litre capacity ice cream maker and a candy thermometer

FOR THE BUTTERSCOTCH

3 tablespoons double cream

1 tablespoon whisky

1 teaspoon Maldon or another flaky sea salt

¼ vanilla bean, split lengthwise

55g plus 1½ tablespoons granulated sugar

4 tablespoons unsalted butter

2 tablespoons packed light brown sugar

1½ teaspoons light corn syrup

FOR THE ICE CREAM

3 medium ears corn, shucked

480ml double cream

225ml whole milk

(continued on next page)

liquid that may be hiding in them, and discard the cobs. Strain the remaining mixture through a sieve into a clean medium pot, stirring and pressing on the kernels to release as much corn flavour as possible. Discard the kernels.

Bring the milk mixture to a simmer over medium heat and turn off the heat. Combine the egg yolks and the remaining 110g of sugar in a medium mixing bowl and whisk until smooth. Slowly but steadily add about 10 tablespoons of the milk mixture to the yolk mixture, whisking constantly. Then slowly but steadily add the yolk mixture to the pot, again whisking constantly. Cook over medium-low heat, whisking constantly and adjusting the heat if necessary to maintain a simmer, until the mixture thickens enough to coat the back of a spoon, about 10 minutes.

Strain the mixture again through a sieve into a medium mixing bowl, pressing and then discarding the solids. Fill a larger bowl halfway with very icy water and nestle the medium bowl inside. Stir frequently until the mixture is cold. Cover the medium bowl and chill in the fridge for at least 4 hours or overnight.

Pour the mixture into an ice cream maker and process according to the manufacturer's instructions. Transfer the ice cream to an airtight container and freeze until firm. Serve straightaway or keep the ice cream in the freezer for up to 3 days.

When you're ready to eat, scoop the ice cream into bowls, drizzle on some butterscotch, and top with some of the caramel popcorn.

¼ teaspoon sea salt

165g granulated sugar

6 large egg yolks

FOR SERVING
Caramel Popcorn with Nuts (page 246), optional

# simple things
## corn

American corn, whether it's white, yellow or bicoloured, is some of the best you can eat: not just candy sweet but full of flavour. Truly lovely corn is one of the pleasures I hadn't experienced until I moved to the States.

Selecting corn can be a bit difficult: pesky husks hide the rows of kernels underneath, so how are you to tell if you've got a good ear? I get a bit grumpy when I see people at the market tearing husks off corn like they own the ears. That's a bit bold, isn't it? The better way is to look for ears whose husks hug the kernels tight. I don't mind if there's a little brown on the silk peeking out at the tip. Run your hands along the husk, feeling the kernels underneath. Not only should the kernels feel nice and firm, none of them dented or missing, but they should also run all the way to the top of the cob. Once you buy your corn, cook it straightaway. Like peas, corn gets starchier and starchier and less and less sweet once picked.

Corn shows up in soup and pudding and pasta in this book. Yet when I have an armful of ears from the market, I'll often go an even simpler route. I'll leave the husks on and soak the corn in a bucket of water for about 15 minutes. I'll get some coals glowing hot and lay the ears directly on the grill grates, husk and all, so the kernels steam. When the husks begin to burn away, the fire licks the kernels and adds a kiss of smokiness. This usually takes 10 to 15 minutes. (If the kernels shrivel up at all, though, it's been too long.) Next, I strip off the husks, rub the corn with butter and sprinkle on salt and perhaps a little lemon juice. Oh – and I always make sure that butter is soft. The softer it is, the faster I get to eat the corn.

# three vegetable juices

When I crave vegetables as a snack rather than as part of a meal, I either gnaw on a carrot or break out my juicer. Vegetable juices are healthy, sure, but I love them for the same reason I do butter and cream, kidneys and marrow: because they taste great. Invest in a high-quality juicer, like a Breville (and the masticating kind if you like green juice), and use these three recipes as jumping-off points. You might want to add a sneaky bit of jalapeño or garlic, or mess around with the proportions to suit your tastes. Tweak them all you want, just promise you'll drink them cold, cold, cold. They're so refreshing that way.

# MY FAVOURITE GREEN JUICE

serves 2

Generous 110g Tuscan kale (about 6 large leaves), very bottoms of stems trimmed, roughly chopped

110g Swiss chard (about 6 large leaves with stems), very bottoms of stems trimmed, roughly chopped

1 green apple (about 225g), washed well, unpeeled, cored and cut into pieces to fit in your juicer

2 large celery stalks, very bottoms trimmed, roughly chopped

A five-finger pinch of basil leaves

A five-finger pinch of mint leaves

A five-finger pinch of delicate flat-leaf parsley sprigs

2 teaspoons lemon juice

Pinch of Maldon or another flaky sea salt

Juice all the ingredients, except the lemon and salt, according to the manufacturer's instructions. To get the maximum amount of juice, you might want to alternate feeding greens and apple through the juicer. Skim off most of the foam. Stir in the lemon juice and salt until the salt dissolves. Pour the juice into two ice-filled glasses and drink straightaway.

# CARROT-ORANGE JUICE WITH GINGER AND CORIANDER

serves 2

Scant 450g (about 2 large), well scrubbed, unpeeled

15g ginger (a 2.5 x 2.5-cm knob), washed well, unpeeled

A five-finger pinch of delicate coriander sprigs

3 tennis-ball-size oranges, halved and squeezed through a strainer into a bowl

One ingredient by one, feed the carrots, ginger and coriander through the juicer. Combine the carrot-juice mixture with the orange juice and stir well. Pour into two ice-filled glasses and drink straightaway.

# BEETROOT-APPLE JUICE

serves 2

Scant 450g beetroot (about
4 medium), washed well,
unpeeled and cut into pieces
to fit in your juicer

1 green apple (about 225g),
washed well, unpeeled, cored
and cut into pieces to fit in your
juicer

Feed the beetroot through the juicer, then the apple. Pour the juice
into two ice-filled glasses and drink straightaway.

*three vegetable juices* **221**

Sauces, dressings, pickles and friends

☆ Kimchi ☆

ment in the fridge
for 2-4 weeks

# CABBAGE KIMCHI

Vicky Oh used to be a kitchen assistant at Salvation Taco. Her family runs its own kimchi company, Arirang, which makes a very tasty version of the pickled vegetable that is Korea's national dish. For my Steamed and Raw Radish Salad with Kimchi and Sesame (page 87), I'll often use a jar of Arirang kimchi. But I got curious about the process of making it myself and just had to have a go at it. I based this recipe on one Vicky shared with me. Turns out it's good fun, slathering a paste of sticky-rice flour, salted shrimp and ground Korean chilli on cabbage leaves and scrunching the heads – particularly when you enlist some friends to help. My theory on kimchi is that if you go through the task of making it, you might as well end up with a lot. Once it's ready, you can give those friends a jar for their efforts.

I like tasting the kimchi at different stages, from the time it's fresh and crunchy all the way until it gets funky and even a bit fizzy. I also like including other farmers' market finds, from all types of radishes to cucumbers to garlic scapes.

Put the cabbage in a big bowl and sprinkle the salt in between the cabbage leaves. Cover and keep in the fridge overnight.

The next day, remove the cabbage from the fridge and drain it well.

Combine the rice flour and 335ml of water in a small pot, whisk until smooth, then set the pot over medium-low heat. Cook, whisking constantly, until the mixture thickens to a loose sludge, 1 to 2 minutes. Take the pot off the heat and let the mixture cool to room temperature.

Combine the gochugaru, garlic, ginger, salted shrimp, sugar and rice flour mixture in a food processor and process until the mixture is smooth. Put the chilli paste in a very large mixing bowl along with the daikon and spring onions. Use gloved hands to mix all three together very well.

Take one of the cabbage quarters and add it to the bowl. Using gloved hands again, slather the vegetable-chilli mixture all over the

SPECIAL EQUIPMENT

A pair of disposable food prep gloves and 3 wide-mouth 2-litre glass or plastic containers with airtight lids, cleaned well

2 large heads Chinese leaf, bottoms trimmed but kept intact, outermost leaves discarded, and quartered lengthwise

About 2 tablespoons Maldon or another flaky sea salt

30g sweet rice flour (also called sticky rice or glutinous rice flour)

180g gochugaru (Korean chilli flakes)

About 20 peeled garlic cloves

50g fresh ginger (an 8 x 4-cm knob), peeled and very roughly sliced

100g jarred Korean salted shrimp (from the refrigerated section of Korean markets)

55g granulated sugar

(continued on next page)

cabbage, spreading it on and between the leaves. Tuck an especially healthy amount into the spaces between the leaves near the bottom of the cabbage. Once the entire cabbage quarter has a red tint, move on to the next one.

Fold the cabbage quarters onto themselves to create tight bundles and divide them among the containers, firmly pressing so they sit tight and leaving at least 2.5cm of space between the cabbage and the jars' openings. Divide any remaining chilli-vegetable mixture among the jars. Press down firmly on the cabbage again to minimise air pockets that might be hiding out.

Seal the jars tightly with the lids and leave them at room temperature overnight. You might want to set them on plates to catch any liquid that sneaks out of the lids as the kimchi ferments. You can nibble on the kimchi at this point, when it's fresh, or keep it in the fridge and eat it after 2 to 4 weeks when it's good and funky. If necessary, occasionally press down on the cabbage with a clean spoon to make sure it's covered by liquid. It'll keep for up to several months.

900g daikon radish, peeled, topped, tailed and cut into 8cm x 3mm matchsticks

450g spring onions (about 5 bunches), roots trimmed, whites and greens trimmed of ugly bits, cut into 2.5-cm lengths

{ the kimchi squat }

# GIARDINIERA

From the Italian word for gardener, *giardiniera* refers to this pickle, a garden's worth of vegetables in a simple brine. The different textures and flavours they provide make for an exciting pickle. The particular vegetables and proportions are ultimately up to you, but I do urge you to seek out Nocellara olives, which are fleshy and not too salty. They keep the giardiniera nice and fresh. Serve it for nibbling with drinks or as part of an antipasti plate. Or finely chop the vegetables, mix in a little dill and spoon it onto hot dogs or sausages, along with a little mustard. The giardiniera keeps in the fridge for a few weeks, but if you like pickles, they won't last that long before they disappear.

Combine the sea salt and 1.8 litres of cold water in a large container and stir to dissolve the salt. Add 2 large handfuls of ice cubes, then the peppers, celery, carrot, onion, cauliflower, radishes, garlic and chillies. Cover and store in the fridge overnight or up to 24 hours.

Drain the vegetables, discarding the water, and rinse them briefly under running water. Drain them very well and pat them dry.

Meanwhile, combine the sugar and 400ml of water in a small pot and set it over medium heat. Cook, stirring frequently, just until the sugar dissolves. Transfer the mixture to a large bowl and add the vinegar, olives, olive brine, oil, oregano and red pepper flakes.

If you have a jar large enough to hold the liquid and vegetables as well as space for the jar in your fridge, go ahead and combine everything in the jar. If not, divide the liquid and vegetables between several tall containers with tight-fitting lids, making sure the liquid covers the veg.

Let it pickle in the fridge for at least 1 week or up to 3 weeks before you eat it. I like it cold or at room temperature. Stir well before you eat.

**makes about 2 litres**

110g sea salt

2 medium red peppers, seeded and deribbed, cut into 2.5-cm pieces

2 medium celery stalks, topped, tailed and cut on the diagonal into 0.5-cm thick slices

1 medium carrot, cut into irregular 2.5-cm pieces

1 medium red onion (about 225g), root trimmed but left intact, peeled and cut into 8 wedges through the root nub

100g small (about 2.5cm) cauliflower florets

100g trimmed medium red radishes, halved lengthwise

1 large head garlic, unpeeled and halved crosswise

2 medium jalapeño chillies, sliced into 0.5-cm thick rings (including seeds)

2 tablespoons granulated sugar

900ml champagne vinegar or white wine vinegar

180g roughly chopped pitted Nocellara olives, plus 225ml of their brine

110ml cup extra-virgin olive oil

1 tablespoon dried oregano

2 teaspoons red pepper flakes

# SPICY DILL PICKLES

At home – unlike in restaurants or on farms – you don't often find yourself flush with barrels of cucumbers that need to be preserved in the cupboard for months and months. So these pickles don't require canning jars or sterilising, because they're meant to last just a few weeks in the refrigerator. This means they're a bit simpler to make. They provide everything you want in a pickle: they're assertively salty and sour, with just a spot of sugar (but not sweetness) for balance. They're plenty crunchy, too – what a shame it would be to lose the texture that makes small cucumbers so good. To that end, always start with cucumbers that are no less than perfect, firm and unblemished. The pickle jar isn't meant to hide rubbish vegetables but rather to preserve nice ones. And don't toss the brine once you've eaten all the pickles. While the pickles are the main event, the flavourful brine makes a fine chaser for a shot of whisky.

Combine the vinegar, salt, sugar, coriander seeds, fennel seeds, mustard seeds and 450ml of water in a medium pot. Set the pot over high heat and bring to a boil, stirring occasionally, until the salt and sugar have dissolved. Remove the mixture from the heat and let it fully cool.

Put the cucumbers, onion, garlic, chillies, dill, thyme and bay leaves in a 2-litre jar or divide them among two tall 1-litre jars. Pour in just enough of the vinegar mixture to cover the cucumbers (you might have a little liquid left over), doing your best to distribute the coriander, fennel and mustard seeds evenly if you're using more than one container.

Cover with an airtight lid and let the cucumbers pickle in the fridge for at least 1 week, or even better 2 weeks, before you eat them. They'll keep for another 2 weeks in the fridge. I like to eat them cold or at room temperature.

**makes about 2 litres**

650ml distilled white vinegar

55g sea salt

3 tablespoons granulated sugar

1 tablespoon coriander seeds

1 tablespoon fennel seeds

1 tablespoon yellow mustard seeds

10 small cucumbers (about 12 x 4cm), halved lengthwise

½ medium Spanish onion, cut into 0.5-cm slices

4 medium garlic cloves, peeled

9 dried red Thai chillies, or arbol chillies

3 large dill sprigs

1 large thyme sprig

3 fresh bay leaves

# PICCALILLI

Food lore has it that piccalilli started as Brits having a go at making achar, Indian-style pickles. I suppose that accounts for the turmeric and ginger. Otherwise, I think we might've missed the target. Personally, I like to think of piccalilli as England's answer to bread and butter pickles. Piccalilli has a similar sweet and sour quality, which I just love. As a kid, I'd dump it on my butter-slathered cheese sandwiches, eat it with sausage rolls or a ploughman's, and wolf it straight from the jar with yellow-stained fingers. My favourite bit was crunching on the little onions, so tiny and perfect. Today I'll still have it on cheese sandwiches made with sharp, funky cheddar, or alongside pâté or boiled ham.

Combine the salt and 1.8 litres of water in a large container and stir to dissolve the salt. Add the cauliflower, cucumbers and onions. Cover and store in the fridge overnight or up to 24 hours.

Drain the vegetables, discarding the water, and rinse them briefly under running water. Let the vegetables sit in the colander for 10 minutes or so, so they drain really well.

Meanwhile, combine the vinegar, sugar, mustard powder and ground ginger in a medium pot. Bring the mixture to a boil over high heat, stirring to dissolve the sugar and spices, then add the vegetables, let the liquid come to a simmer, and lower the heat to maintain a gentle simmer. Cook just until the onions give slightly when you squeeze them, about 4 minutes. Drain the vegetables in a sieve set over a large bowl, reserving the liquid, and return the liquid to the pot.

Bring the liquid to a boil once more, whisk in the flour and turmeric, and whisk for a minute or so. Working in batches, blend the mixture (be careful when blending hot liquids) until smooth.

If you have a jar large enough to hold the liquid and vegetables as

**makes 2 generous litres**

110g sea salt

1 small head cauliflower, cut into 4-cm florets

5 small crunchy cucumbers without big seeds, peeled and cut into irregularly shaped 4-cm pieces

300g small pickling onions, soaked in warm water, peeled and trimmed of any tough bits

1.3 litres distilled white vinegar

110g granulated sugar

1 tablespoon mustard powder (preferably Colman's)

1 teaspoon ground ginger

55g plain flour

3½ tablespoons ground turmeric

well as space for the jar in your fridge, go ahead and combine everything in the jar. If not, divide the liquid and vegetables among several tall containers with tight-fitting lids, making sure the liquid covers the veg. Let everything cool fully, then cover with the lids and refrigerate.

Let the piccalilli pickle in the fridge for at least 2 days before you eat it. It keeps in the fridge for up to 3 weeks more. I like to eat it cold or at room temperature.

# CARROT-TOP PESTO

If you've never nibbled a carrot top, you have a happy surprise waiting for you. The greens are delicious: a little less carroty than the roots, and almost briny, like heartier borage. Arriving home from the market with not only a collection of sweet, colourful roots but also a big old tuft of bushy tops is like ordering pork shoulder and finding out that the kind butcher has snuck a couple of trotters into your bag.

I treat the tops as I would a tender herb, adding little sprigs to salads as I might parsley or dill. And because each bunch of carrots can bring twice the volume in tops, I make pesto. As much as I like the particular flavour of the tops themselves, I also like how they carry the flavour of basil, which comes through quite a bit considering how few leaves you use.

Combine the carrot tops and basil in a small food processor, pulse several times, then add the walnuts, Parmesan, garlic and salt. Pulse several more times, add the oil, then process full-on, stopping and scraping down the sides of the processor or stirring gently if need be, until the mixture is well combined but still a bit chunky. Taste and season with more salt, if you fancy.

makes about 275g

100g delicate carrot tops (stems discarded), roughly chopped

A small handful of basil leaves

55g walnut halves

25g Parmesan cheese, finely grated

1 medium garlic clove, halved lengthwise

1 teaspoon Maldon or another flaky sea salt

110ml extra-virgin olive oil

# KALE PURÉE

If it weren't for Kale Purée, I wouldn't be where I am today. I was still a young cook in England wondering what I'd do next when I saw Rose Gray and Ruth Rogers, chefs at London's River Café, on the telly. At the time, food TV wasn't all clever editing and pretty colours. Their show on the BBC just showed them, cooking. I watched them make this four-ingredient purée and toss it in a pan with some penne. They were accomplished chefs, but the food they were making wasn't complicated at all. I wanted to cook like that. So I called up River Café and talked my way into a tryout. I went on to work there, and Rose and Ruth became my mentors and friends. I'm grateful that they never tried my first go at the purée, which I made immediately after I switched off the telly. I used crap olive oil and it wasn't very good. Please don't make the mistake I did.

Put 4 of the garlic cloves in a medium pot, fill it with water, cover, and bring the water to a boil over high heat. Add enough sea salt so that the water tastes slightly salty and add the kale, prodding to submerge it. Cook uncovered until the kale is tender and tears easily, 2 to 3 minutes.

Fish out the boiled garlic cloves from the pot and reserve them. Drain the kale in a colander and when it's cool enough to handle, squeeze out as much water as you can. Roughly chop the kale, the boiled garlic and the raw garlic.

Combine the kale, garlic and Maldon salt in a food processor. Process, stopping occasionally to prod and stir, for about 45 seconds, then add the oil and process, stirring once or twice, to a fairly smooth purée. Whenever I make this at one of my restaurants, I use a Vita-Prep to make the purée silky smooth, but I like a slightly coarse purée too.

The purée keeps in an airtight container in the fridge for up to 5 days.

**makes about 225g**

5 medium garlic cloves, peeled

450g Tuscan kale, thick stems removed (about 225g after trimming)

Sea salt

1 teaspoon Maldon or another flaky sea salt

110ml extra-virgin olive oil

A NEAT TRICK
FOR REMOVING KALE STEMS

Before I use kale or other leafy greens with woody stems, I often remove the thick stems. I've seen home cooks do this with a knife, which you can do if you fancy. I have a quicker way. Working one leaf at a time, firmly grab the end of the stem with one hand. With the other, use your thumb and index finger to firmly pinch together the bottom of the leaf on either side of the stem and pull away from the stem end, stripping off the leaves in one go.

# GRILLED-VEGETABLE VINAIGRETTE

I like salads that keep you occupied, that give you something to search for and get excited about. This chunky dressing brings that pleasure to even the simplest salad. Thanks to the dressing, each bite of the salad is different. You might come across a sweet bit of fennel or onion in one bite, and a slightly bitter bit of Treviso in another. Bright with vinegar and herbs, the dressing also goes well spooned over a steak along with crumbled blue cheese or dolloped on a lamb chop with some feta.

Halve the fennel bulb lengthwise and cut each half through the root nub (so the wedges stay intact) into approximately 2.5-cm thick wedges.

Heat a grill or heavy grill pan over high heat until it's good and hot, about 5 minutes. Reduce the heat to medium and add the fennel, onion and Treviso. Cook, turning the vegetables over occasionally, until the fennel and onion are lightly charred in spots and cooked through, but still have a little bite, about 20 minutes. The Treviso is done when the stems are tender but still have a little bite, the leaves are wilty, the tips crackly, and the colour has changed from magenta to sienna with dark brown edges, 15 to 20 minutes.

As they finish, pop the grilled vegetables into a bowl and cover with clingfilm until they've cooled fully. They'll steam a bit and cook some more as they cool. Once they've all cooled, chop the vegetables into a mix of about 1-cm pieces, some smaller and some larger.

Pop the vegetables back into the bowl, add the oil, vinegar, salt and garlic, and stir really well. Toss the mint and marjoram together on a cutting board, give them a rough chop, and stir them into the dressing.

makes about 450ml

1 medium fennel bulb, outer layer, stalks and fronds removed, root end trimmed of brown bits

1 small red onion (about 110g), cut into 1-cm thick rounds

1 small head Treviso (a generous 110g), outermost leaves removed, bottom trimmed of brown bits, quartered lengthwise, or a small head radicchio, prepped like the Treviso and cut into 1-cm thick wedges

110ml extra-virgin olive oil

3 tablespoons sherry vinegar

1 teaspoon Maldon or another flaky sea salt

1 small garlic clove, very finely chopped

A five-finger pinch of mint leaves

A five-finger pinch of marjoram leaves

# SALAD CREAM

This creamy, tangy dressing is meant to mimic the bottled salad cream I grew up with in England, which I poured all over raw vegetables. I realise now that it's a lot like a really liquidy version of the deviled egg filling I make at the Spotted Pig, with a little tarragon thrown in. If you're making this for Salad Sandwiches (page 84), you might want to give some of the boiled egg whites a good old chop and pile them on the bread along with the soft-boiled eggs. No point in wasting.

Fill a medium pot at least halfway with water and bring it to a boil over high heat. Use a slotted spoon to gently add the eggs to the water, cook them for 10 minutes (set a timer), then run them under cold water until they're fully cool. Lightly tap each egg against the counter to crack the shell all over, then peel them, halve them lengthwise, and pop out the yolks. (Reserve the whites for another purpose, like Salad Sandwiches, or for nibbling.)

Use the back of a spoon to force the yolks through a mesh sieve into a food processor. Add the oil, cream, vinegar, mustard, garlic, salt, and 2 teaspoons of water and process until very smooth and creamy. Add the tarragon and process briefly. It keeps in an airtight container in the refrigerator for up to 2 days.

makes about 225ml

6 large eggs

55ml extra-virgin olive oil

60ml double cream

2 tablespoons red wine vinegar

1 tablespoon plus 1 teaspoon Dijon mustard

1 very small garlic clove, roughly chopped

1 teaspoon Maldon or another flaky sea salt

A small handful of tarragon leaves, roughly chopped

# SIMPLE LEMON DRESSING

This all-purpose dressing brightens whatever it touches, like Sugar Snap Pea Salad (page 23) or Greek Salad (page 81). It proves that three modest ingredients can become something extra-special when they're combined in just the right proportions.

Combine the ingredients in a container with a tight-fitting lid and shake well until the mixture looks creamy. Taste and add a little more oil, lemon or salt, if you'd like. Set it aside until you're ready to use it and shake again just before you do.

**makes about 165ml**

110ml extra-virgin olive oil

55ml lemon juice

¾ teaspoon Maldon or another flaky sea salt

# RED ZA'ATAR SPICE

Many Middle Eastern cooks have their own family recipe for this classic spice blend. This is my version. While some cooks use dried herbs and only a little sumac, I like to use fresh herbs, like thyme and marjoram, and lots of sumac, which gives the za'atar a pretty purplish red colour and a refreshing lemony quality. The mixture is meant to season Vegetable Crisps (page 200), but it's also a fine thing to sprinkle on thick yogurt or douse with olive oil to make a dip for bread.

Toast the sesame seeds in a small dry cast-iron frying pan over medium-low heat, stirring and tossing almost constantly, just until they've turned a light golden colour, 1 to 2 minutes. Transfer them to a bowl to cool.

Combine the sumac and herbs in a small food processor (or small spice grinder) and process to a fairly fine, slightly moist powder. Put the mixture in the bowl with the sesame seeds, add the salt and stir well.

The za'atar keeps in an airtight container in the fridge for up to 5 days.

**makes about 110g**

1 tablespoon sesame seeds

25g sumac

2 tablespoons very coarsely chopped marjoram leaves

2 tablespoons very coarsely chopped oregano leaves

2 tablespoons very coarsely chopped thyme leaves

½ teaspoon Maldon or another flaky sea salt

# MY GARAM MASALA

Any Indian grocer and many supermarkets nowadays stock this spice mixture, which is a staple in Indian cooking. But premade versions aren't quite as nice as those you make yourself. When you toast and grind whole spices, the resulting mixture is especially lively and aromatic. While a spice grinder is much easier on your arm, I prefer using a mortar to make the coarse powder, because the smell of toasty pulverised spices is so invigorating. In fact, if you do, you might want to whack the cardamom pods with the flat of a chef's knife, discard the fibrous pods and use just the seeds.

Combine the coriander, cumin, cardamom, cinnamon, chillies, mace and cloves in a medium cast-iron frying pan. Set the pan over medium-low heat and cook, shaking and tossing frequently, until the spices are toasty and very fragrant, about 5 minutes. Transfer them to a bowl or plate to cool slightly, then grind them to a coarse powder in a spice grinder or pound them in a large mortar. Add the nutmeg, ground ginger and bay leaves, and grind or pound until you have a fairly fine powder. It's OK if the bay leaves are still in small pieces and not completely broken down.

Store the garam masala in an airtight container in a cool, dry place for up to 1 month.

**makes about 125g**

3 tablespoons coriander seeds

3 tablespoons cumin seeds

1 tablespoon green cardamom pods

2 small cinnamon sticks (about 8cm each), roughly crumbled

10 dried pequín chillies, crumbled, or pinches of red pepper flakes

½ whole mace blade or 1 teaspoon pieces

2 teaspoons whole cloves

1½ tablespoons finely grated nutmeg (from about 2 small nutmegs)

2 teaspoons ground ginger

2 large fresh bay leaves, stems removed and leaves torn into small pieces

# SIMPLE TOMATO SAUCE

As with so many seemingly simple things, decent tomato sauce is easy to make, but good tomato sauce is not. I thought I could make good tomato sauce until I started working at the River Café, where I met a guy called Joseph Travelli. Everyone called him 'Steam Train' Travelli, because he was well known for zipping around corners, a dangerous habit in any kitchen. I came to know him best for his knack with tomato sauce. His tasted so much better than mine that I quickly realised I was still at square one, and I decided to try to crack the code on Travelli's method. Lucky me, I got to watch him make tomato sauce again and again. As far as I could tell, the two most important components to his sauce were the tomatoes and the garlic. The tomatoes must be top-quality, whether you're using fresh or tinned. The better they are, the better the result. That's obvious. Not so obvious is the role of garlic. Steam Train might not have known how to turn a corner with grace, but he had a way with garlic. He browned it just enough to bring out the most warmth and umami, which would permeate the tomatoes and turn the sauce into something special. I follow his lead here, paying particularly close attention to the sizzling garlic. And since this is a book on veg, I figured that I should leave out the guanciale that adds a porky, funky flavour to some of my favourite tomato sauces. Instead, I use red onions, which give the sauce a meatiness that regular onions don't.

Working with one at a time, hold the tomatoes over a bowl and use a finger to poke through the flesh and squeeze gently so the liquid inside spills into the bowl. Strain and reserve the liquid and roughly chop the tomatoes.

Heat 3 tablespoons of the oil in a medium pot over medium-high heat until it shimmers. Add the onion and 1 teaspoon of the salt. Lower the heat to medium and cook the onions at a steady sizzle, stirring occasionally, until they go translucent, 4 to 5 minutes.

**makes about 450ml**

4 x 400g tins whole tomatoes, drained and trimmed (see page 16)

4 tablespoons extra-virgin olive oil

1 medium red onion (225g), finely diced

1½ teaspoons Maldon or another flaky sea salt

2 medium garlic cloves, thinly sliced

A five-finger pinch of basil leaves, roughly chopped at the last minute

Push the onion to one side of the pot and add the garlic to the oil. Pay especially close attention to the garlic as you cook, stirring the garlic occasionally but not the onion, until the slices turn a light golden colour and smell toasty, about 3 minutes. Stir it all together with the onion and cook, stirring now and then, until the slices turn golden with slightly darker edges, about 5 minutes more. Just when you start to freak out that the edges might begin to burn, stir in the tomatoes (not the liquid just yet).

Raise the heat to medium-high, and let the mixture simmer rapidly, stirring and breaking up the tomatoes a bit, until it looks less like separate bits and more like one sauce, about 3 minutes. Add the tomato liquid, bring it to a vigorous simmer, then lower the heat to maintain a gentle simmer. Cook, stirring now and then, until the sauce thickens slightly and the flavours have a chance to mingle, about 30 minutes.

Stir in the basil, the remaining 1 tablespoon of oil, and the remaining ½ teaspoon of salt. Raise the heat to bring the sauce to a proper simmer and cook until it thickens slightly and you can taste the basil a bit more, about 5 minutes.

Use the sauce right away or let it cool and store it in an airtight container in the fridge for up to 3 days.

# SIMPLE BEANS

It's always nice to have dried beans in your cupboard. Even better is having cooked beans in your fridge, swimming in an earthy, olive-oil-enriched liquor. That way you're always that much closer to a hearty supper, whether you're making Bean and Mushroom Salad (page 92) or Summery Ribollita (page 110), or if you want to turn a simple vegetable dish into a satisfying meal. I like to blend some of the beans with the cooking liquid so the liquor has a little extra body and flavour. This liquor, by the way, is great in soups as a sort of vegetarian stock.

Put the beans in a medium pot with the garlic, oil, and enough water to cover them by a couple of centimetres. Set the pot over medium-high heat and bring the liquid to a simmer. Lower the heat to maintain a gentle simmer and cook until the beans are tender and almost creamy inside but before they start bursting, 1 to 2 hours, depending on the freshness of your beans. Stir in the salt, turn off the heat, and let the beans sit for about 15 minutes in the liquid until they're fully creamy.

Fish out the garlic cloves and add them to a blender along with a few cups of the cooking liquid and 75g of the beans. Blend until smooth, pour the mixture into the pot, and have a gentle stir. The beans keep in their liquid in the fridge for several days.

**makes about 1.75kg of beans and liquid**

450g high-quality dried borlotti, cannellini or similar beans, picked over, soaked overnight in water and drained

1 large head garlic, cloves separated and peeled

110ml extra-virgin olive oil

1 tablespoon plus 1 teaspoon Maldon or another flaky sea salt

# SIMPLE CHICKEN STOCK

I don't like to think of meat and vegetables as playing for two separate teams. They're more like good friends, each helping out the other on occasion. That's why I put a recipe for chicken stock in a book on veg. It provides a unique richness and depth to Potato Soup with Garlic and Parsley (page 62), Spring Egg Drop Soup (page 38) and Braised Peas and Little Gem Lettuce (page 24). Even though all three dishes remain focused on the flavour of vegetables, none would be as tasty without the stock in the background. Now and then as it bubbles away, I like to fish out bits of meat from the crannies of the bones, sprinkle on a little salt and have a nibble. Even though making stock doesn't take much work, you still deserve a reward.

Put all the ingredients in a large pot and bring to a vigorous simmer over high heat. Don't let it boil or you'll end up with a cloudy stock. Reduce the heat so the water simmers only very gently and cook, skimming the gunk off the surface but resisting the urge to stir, for about 4 hours. Along the way, tweak the heat if you need to, so little bubbles just break the surface here and there. After 4 hours or so it should be ready, but give it a taste – you want it to taste like chicken. If it doesn't, let it simmer a bit longer. Once it's good and tasty, strain the stock through a fine-mesh sieve into a large pot or bowl and discard the solids.

If you mean to use the stock straightaway, skim off the clear fat with a spoon. If not, let the stock come to room temperature, then cover and chill the stock until the fat rises to the surface and solidifies. Scrape off the white fat and keep the stock in the refrigerator for up to 3 days or in the freezer for up to a month.

makes about 3 litres

2.2kg chicken bones, such as backs, wings and necks, cut into big chunks by your butcher

1 large Spanish onion (about 450g), peeled and quartered

1 medium carrot, peeled, topped, tailed and halved lengthwise

3 medium celery stalks, halved crosswise

1 garlic head, unpeeled and halved crosswise

20 or so black peppercorns

2 small fresh bay leaves

1 small thyme sprig

4 litres water

# CARAMEL POPCORN WITH NUTS

A fantastic topping for Sweet-Corn Ice Cream (page 213), this caramel corn also makes for great snacking. Fair warning: it's dangerous, this stuff. If the crunchy, sweet, salty mixture is within 50 feet, I'm drawn to it like a pig to mud.

Besides the pleasure of munching each handful, making the popcorn is silly fun: in case you forgot, it's just about the coolest thing ever. In go the golden kernels, then after a ruckus under the lid, out comes fluffy white popped corn. You can buy popping corn any time of year, though in the dead of winter spotting a bag of kernels on a farmer's table makes for an extra-bright spot in a dark time. Even the most humble vegetables, in the most barren of seasons, can bring a bit of magic.

Position a rack in the centre of the oven and preheat to 150°C/gas 2. Line a baking sheet with baking parchment.

Spread the nuts on the baking sheet and bake, stirring occasionally, until the nuts are a shade or two darker and very aromatic, about 15 minutes. Transfer the nuts to a large mixing bowl and loosely cover with foil to keep warm. Leave the oven on and the paper on the baking sheet.

Add the oil to a heavy pot large enough to hold a large bowl of popped popcorn. Heat the oil over medium-high heat until it begins to smoke. Add the kernels and cover the pot. Once you hear the first kernels pop, position the lid so some air can escape and steady it with one hand, and with the other shake the pot vigorously until the pops are about 2 seconds apart. Put the popcorn in the bowl with the nuts and keep in a warm place, such as near the oven.

Combine the brown sugar, maple syrup, corn syrup and butter in a medium saucepan. Attach a candy thermometer and bring the mixture to a vigorous simmer over medium-high heat. Let it simmer, without stirring, until the mixture reaches 120°C/180°F. Add the salt, vanilla

**makes a large bowlful**

SPECIAL EQUIPMENT
A candy thermometer

110g unsalted roasted peanuts

110g pecan halves

55g blanched hazelnuts

1 tablespoon neutral oil, such as canola or grapeseed

50g popcorn kernels

110g packed light brown sugar

55ml plus 2 tablespoons pure maple syrup

55ml plus 2 tablespoons light corn syrup

50g unsalted butter

1½ teaspoons sea salt

½ teaspoon vanilla extract

⅛ teaspoon bicarbonate of baking soda

extract and baking soda, and have one good stir. The mixture will froth. Immediately pour it over the popcorn and nuts, and stir to coat everything well.

Spread the mixture in an even layer onto the paper-lined baking sheet. Pop it in the oven and bake, stirring occasionally, until the popcorn is barely sticky to the touch and crunchy, about 30 minutes. Let it cool to room temperature and break up the clusters a bit, if you'd like.

It keeps in an airtight container at room temperature for up to 3 days.

# *index*

NOTE: Page references in *italics* refer to photos.

## A

anchovies
  about, 13–14
  Piedmontese Peppers with
    Tomato, Basil and Anchovy,
    *106,* 107
  Whole Pot-Roasted Cauliflower
    with Tomatoes and
    Anchovies, 66–67, *68*
Artichokes with White Wine and
  Capers, Pot-Roasted, *30,*
  31–32, *33*
asparagus
  Asparagus Quiches with Mint,
    *43,* 44–46, *47*
  Boiled Asparagus with Ramp
    Béarnaise Sauce, *34,* 35–37
  Tagliatelle with Asparagus and
    Parmesan Fonduta, *132,* 133
Aubergine Caponata, If-It-Ain't-
  Broke, 100–101, *102*
Aubergine with Ground Pork and
  Thai Basil, Steamed, 171

autumn recipes. *see* chilly weather
  treats

## B

Baby Turnips, Roasted Whole, *72,*
  73–74
Batali, Mario, 156
Bean and Mushroom Salad, *91,*
  92–93
Beans, Simple, 244
beast recipes. *see* meat recipes
Beetroot-Apple Juice, 221
Beetroot, Stems and Greens,
  Boiled, 76–77
Bitter Leaves with Pomegranate
  and Grilled-Vegetable
  Vinaigrette, 80
Boiled Asparagus with Ramp
  Béarnaise Sauce, *34,* 35–37
Boiled Potatoes with Butter and
  Mint, *52,* 53
Braised Collards with Bacon,
  Vinegar and Chillies, *168,*
  169–170

# about the author

**APRIL BLOOMFIELD** is the executive chef and co-owner of the Michelin-starred the Spotted Pig, the Breslin, the John Dory, Tosca and Salvation Taco restaurants. She won the 2014 James Beard Award for Best Chef in New York and was nominated for an Emmy for co-hosting the second season of the PBS show *Mind of a Chef*. A native of Birmingham, England, she lives in New York City.

thank you